L

Travel Guide

101 Unique, Interesting, & Fun Places to Visit, Explore, and Experience Denver Colorado to the Fullest from A to Z

HowExpert with Caitlyn Knuth

For more tips related to this topic, visit www.HowExpert.com/travel.

Recommended Resources

www.HowExpert.com – Quick 'How To' Guides on Unique Topics by Everyday Experts.

www.HowExpert.com/writers - Write About Your #1 Passion/Knowledge/Experience.

www.HowExpert.com/membership - Learn a New 'How To' Topic About Practically Everything Every Week.

www.HowExpert.com/jobs - Check Out HowExpert Jobs.

Table of Contents

Recommended Resources 2
Chapter 1: Destination Denver 8
Colorado Calling: A Blank Canvas for New Life 8
Chapter 2: Finding Your Way Through Flavor:
Restaurant Must-Stops 16
For Fun and People Watching 16
   Next Door Community Pub 16
   Tap Fourteen Rooftop Beer Garden 17
   ViewHouse Ballpark 18
   ACME Delicatessen 19
For a Night Out on the Town 20
   Avelina 20
   Morton's, The Steak House 21
   Izakaya Den 22
   Que Bueno Suerte! 23
For Feeling Free 23
   Backcountry Delicatessen 24
   The Wooden Table 25
   Jax Fish House and Oyster Bar 25
   Cuba Cuba Sandwicheria 26
For Your Sweet Tooth 27
   Milk and Cake Yogurt & Cupcakes 27
   Protein Bar & Kitchen 28
   Gateaux Bakery 29
For You Global Gastronomy Needs 29
   Blue Sushi Sake Grill 30
   Rhein Haus 30
   Bistro Vendome Rendezvous Des Amis 31
For Feeling Nostalgic 31
   Public School Restaurant and Bar 32
For When You're Feeling Fancy 33
   Osteria Marco 33
Chapter 3: The Heart of Denver's History 35
Union Station 35
Brown Palace Hotel & Spa 37
Red Rocks Amphitheatre 38
The Daniels and Fisher Tower 39
Molly Brown House Museum 40
The Tattered Cover Bookstore 41
Chapter 4: Denver's Dance Scene 43
The Clocktower Cabaret 43

Black Belt Salsa *44*
Hart's Dancewear *44*
La Rumba *45*
Chapter 5: An Educational Point of View 46
University of Denver Colorado: CU in the City *46*
Metropolitan State University *47*
Chapter 6: Making the Most of Mile High Museums ... 48
Denver Art Museum *48*
Denver Museum of Nature and Science *49*
Wings Over the Rockies Air and Space Museum *50*
Denver Botanic Gardens *51*
Denver Firefighters Museum *52*
Chapter 7: Journey Just Outside Denver 53
Edelweiss *53*
Cheyanne Mountain Zoo *54*
The Rocky Mountain Dinosaur Resource Center *55*
Pueblo Riverwalk *56*
Rocky Mountain National Park *56*
Chapter 8: Parks for One and All 58
City Park *58*
Wallace Park *59*
Cherry Creek State Park *60*
Commons Park *61*
Water World *62*
Ruby Hill Park *62*
Chapter 9: Exclusively for the Kids 64
The Denver Zoo *64*
Children's Museum of Denver *65*
Monster Mini Golf *66*
AMF Monaco Lanes *66*
Jumpstreet *67*
Cave of the Winds *68*
Union Station Fountains *69*
Downtown Aquarium *70*
Elitch Gardens *71*
The Wild Animal Sanctuary *72*
Chapter 10: Top-Notch Shopping Stops 74
16th Street Mall *74*
Larimer Square *75*
Park Meadows Mall *76*
Historic Downtown Littleton *77*
Ikea *78*
Chapter 11: Hotels You Have to See to Believe 80

The Oxford Hotel *80*
The Crawford Hotel *82*
Magnolia Hotel *83*
Chapter 12: Discovering Denver's Coffee Shops 84
Pigtrain Coffee Company *84*
Amante Coffee *85*
Mangiamo Pronto *85*
Novo *86*
Chapter 13: Majestic Mountain Excursions 88
Breckenridge *88*
Vail *89*
Winter Park *90*
Mountain-Bound Groups *91*
Jellystone Park *92*
Chapter 14: Theater, Stage and Performance 94
Paramount Theater *94*
The Denver Performing Arts Complex *95*
Film On The Rocks *96*
88 Drive In Theatre *96*
AMC Highlands Ranch 24 .... *97*
Chapter 15: Venues with a View 99
Inspiration Point Park *99*
Denver International Airport *100*
Peaks Lounge *101*
**Chapter 16: Athletic Intrigue--Denver's Best Sporting
Stops.. 102**
Coors Field-Colorado Rockies *102*
Mile High Stadium-Denver Broncos *103*
Pepsi Center-Denver Nuggets *104*
The REI Denver Flagship Store *105*
Chapter 17: Denver and the Divine 107
Flatirons Community Church *107*
Potter's House Church of Denver *108*
Cathedral Basilica of the Immaculate Conception *109*
Chapter 18: Stopping for a Drink Along the Way 111
Terminal Bar *111*
Thirsty Lion Gastropub & Grill *112*
Falling Rock Tap House *113*
Skyline Beer Garden *114*
Marg's World Taco Bistro *115*
Chapter 19: A Trip Through Colorado Springs 116
Compassion International *116*
United States Air Force Academy *117*

The Broadmoor *118*
Garden of the Gods...*119*
Chapter 20: Seasonal Stops **121**
Downtown Christmas Market...*121*
Parker Trick or Treat on Mainstreet *122*
Anderson Farms... *123*
Chapter 21: Last Minute Tips and Tricks **125**
Being a Mindful Tourist.. *125*
Living with the Lite Rail *126*
About the Expert **128**
Recommended Resources **129**

Chapter 1: Destination Denver

Colorado Calling: A Blank Canvas for New Life

It's human nature to actively travel towards excitement. There are cities that pulse with the adrenaline of humanity and it's thrilling to consider how we might fit into a place where all that is contemporary and cutting edge finds space to collide. Many of us yearn to be a part of those places where we witness culture thriving, opportunity knocking and the possibility of obtaining happiness always within reach.

While it's a far fetch to say that a city in and of itself can inhabit all these enticing characteristics...Denver gets amazingly close. Denver is a daring city where risk and reward run high and the thrill of it all seems to invite newcomers in by the thousands. The evidence that many others take a similar point of view is clear in the ever-growing population boom Denver has been experiencing for the last several years. With an exploding housing market, huge hiring rates and a population as diverse as the natural world that surrounds it, Denver calls to individuals from all walks of life—beckoning them towards something new and refreshing. The city itself markets its boundaries as a place where creativity is born. A blank canvas for starting a brand-new life within the capital boundaries of Colorado. It's a hard pitch to resist.

Maybe it's something in the mountain air that flows over the Front Range, or the thrill of witnessing the wonder that is urban sprawl happening right before your very eyes, but Denver is a city that demands your attention from the moment you first lay eyes on it. Outdoor enthusiasts find themselves captivated by the proximity the city holds to some of the most rugged and adrenaline-inducing terrain. Those whose hearts beat for an urban scene full of fresh music and modern flavors find Denver to be an ever-revolving door of artistic talent and opportunity. Still others flock to the capital of Colorado for a chance to earn a degree at one of the renowned universities Denver hosts city-center.

Progressive, passionate and constantly pursuing the balance between the natural world and the urban center, Denver is a unique city on the map when it comes to discovering places that aim for authenticity. It's not a problem-free city, but that's how people like it. It opens doors for potential solutions customized to the city they are designed for. Where a collective pursuit of something raw, revealing and freeing collides—Denver finds the voice and strength of its siren call.

A City of Growth

Where once upon a time Denver was a place people seemed to move exclusively for the outdoor adventure, today the list of reasons to move to Denver has grown exponentially. Over the past decade, Denver has seen a hike in population like never before. Initially attributed to the legalization of Marijuana alongside a booming demand for workers,

Denver quickly changed from quiet mountainside oasis to bustling urban sprawl of creativity and commerce before its residents' very eyes. As with all change, this has presented it's benefits and pitfalls. The Denver Post reported in March of 2018 that the city had seen nearly 100,000 residents added to its roster in just seven years. With the influx of outsiders came a growing demand for housing options, improved infrastructure, parks and subdivisions.

Where once Denver was simply... Denver, today the city is a virtual patchwork of neighborhoods and suburbs that define themselves as uniquely a part of the larger Denver picture. Downtown Denver has taken on a life of its own with business booming in the financial sectors. Young professionals from across the country are finding a place to thrive within the context of Denver's growth and opportunity. Similarly, construction is a near constant state of being both within the heart of the city and beyond. Places like the Denver Tech Center and suburbs of Highlands Ranch have seen incredible numbers of residential homes, apartment buildings and condos find a place within their boundaries and more seem to be in the works as we speak.

Many long-time Denver residents have found the influx of out-of-towners refreshing, but also challenging where the change concerns housing prices and traffic. In the past five years, Denver residents have seen the cost of living sky rocket, creating a stunning gap in home values and pushing many residents to the outskirts in the name of budget-friendly options. Congestion on the roadways has also become a primary concern for those who now call Denver home. While local government officials furiously work on plans to expand interstates and highways in the name of stress-less commutes, drivers experience long waits and frequent accidents on the primary lanes leading into central Denver.

While there is much to be done in the way of adjustments, Denver is a city open to change and it hosts a population of eclectic and energetic individuals who are pursuing their passions with determination and carrying the tradition of creativity along with them. Those out-of-state license plates you see as you make your way through Denver are a testament to the power and pull of the city. From artists to engineers, financial experts to those who walk on the greener side of life, Denver is a growing city working on making space for everyone now and well into the future.

A Few Things to Know Before You Go

Every city holds close to its heart those few unique clichés that make it both charming and irresistible. Every traveler wants to know if the rumors are true and when it comes to this sentiment, Denver is no exception to the rule.

Assumption #1

In the wake of the legalization of Cannabis in Colorado, many feared the city might transform into a zombie land of leaf-loving enthusiasts. I'm happy to announce that while the Cannabis industry and those individuals associated with it are thriving, the city hasn't lost its sense of self in any sort of all-consuming phenomenon. If you're not used to Marijuana being so freely referenced, a trip to Denver can be a bit shocking but I promise, the surprise quickly passes as you realize that it's a part of life in Denver, but not necessarily a priority. Dispensaries and clinics are built in those same places any other business might be found. Next door to gas stations, across the street from Target or close by cafes, it's not uncommon to see a green logo indicating the business intentions of those inside. For those who are traveling through and haven't witnessed this before, you'll find it to be less intense than previously imagined. Once you realize what you're looking at, you'll soon understand that the advertisements for such establishments are often understated and non-threatening to those who don't partake. In fact, much like other pharmacies, those that provide Cannabis tend to take on a rather generic appearance once you've seen enough of them.

Assumption #2

When it comes to places where pets may possibly outnumber people, Denver reigns supreme. Yes, the rumors on this one are very true. The idea that Denver is made up of dog-first people is one of those clichés that is definitely Denver-accurate. Locals and out-of-towners alike love their dogs and make no apologies about the fact that their canine pals hold the same place in their hearts as most people. It's not uncommon to see residents walking down the street with several leashes in hand. From downtown social scenes to the family-friendly suburbs of the city, dogs make up an important part of most Denver residents' lives. In fact, the dog walking service that goes by the name of Rover has seen incredible success in Denver over the past few years as the population growth occurs on both the human and four-legged friend scale.

Assumption #3

It's easy to assume that Denver's many new residents, incredible job market and excessive housing market would make for a city that's rolling in wealth and opportunity for everyone. Unfortunately, this isn't quite the case. As with many big cities, great growth has also left certain groups of residents out in the cold. Downtown Denver is home to an ever-increasing number of homeless citizens. As the city continues to expand, there is a strain on resources born out of a period of time where many services are frantically playing catch-up in order to meet the new levels of demand. While many of Denver's homeless struggle with unresolved mental health issues, others are part of a unique Urban Camper movement. This group is primarily made up of young adults who have taken to the streets in a conscience act of rebellion against a life of conformity. Unfortunately, this creates a difficult situation for the city of Denver in general as officials work through potential paths towards housing those who need it most and helping others overcome addictions and adverse environments.

Assumption #4

Denver's prime mountainside location frames the Front Range with affection and just beyond those gentle peaks rises the rustic Rocky Mountains. Beckoning to those with a heart for the slopes, many assume that everyone in Denver is taking on Black

Diamonds every snowy weekend they can...and they just might be right. While it's clearly not fair to say that all of Denver skis regularly, a large portion of the population is dedicated to the outdoor world and skiing comes as part of the package deal. Can you blame them? With some of the best runs in the country sitting right outside, it's hard to imagine anyone turning down the chance to take to the mountaintops and try their skills at skiing.

Good news is in store for those who haven't shred the slopes before but want to give it a go in Denver. Nearly every expert here is waiting to pass on tips, tricks and advice to newbies who are heading for the mountains. With enough classes, outdoor groups and individual tour options to fill a book of their own, learning to ski when you're in Denver doesn't have to be a scary or impossible experience. In fact, a ski trip is built on the idea of comradery. There is a social aspect to ski getaways that makes it just as much about the people as the fresh powder. Taking some time for the mountains is a good way to get a sense of local life, and maybe learn some Denver-centric outdoor lingo along the way.

Finding Denver for Yourself

Whether those funny, wacky or weird rumors are true or not doesn't matter so much when you're looking to travel to Denver. Half the fun in discovering a new place is learning how it exists on its own and also becomes a part of your life in a completely unique way. Finding out just what it is that makes Denver so appealing to the masses these days is an adventure worth your while. When you're here, taking in the many sights tends to lead to life-long memories that will have you dreaming of returning before you've even left.

Chapter 2: Finding Your Way Through Flavor: Restaurant Must-Stops

For Fun and People Watching

Denver is a city built on the concept of new horizons and the possibility factor extends into dining establishments as well. From one side of the city to the other, Denver is a destination brimming with delicious opportunities to please your palate and you don't have to look far to find fantastic places to try something new while people watching too! Here are a few of the stops that should definitely be on your must-try list when it comes to passing an afternoon watching the world go by.

Next Door Community Pub

1701 Wynkoop, Suite 100, Denver, Colorado 80202

When you're looking to dine in the diverse Denver we know and love, while maintaining a sense of all-American pride, Next Door Community Pub on Wynkoop is your stop. Serving food entirely sourced from American farms, this casual and tasty locale is attached to the newly renovated Union Station. A fun and airy atmosphere with both indoor and outdoor seating options, you can kick back with a fresh meal adjacent to the stunning and bustling train station or linger outdoors in the sunshine and take in the downtown vibe via patio.

The menu includes everything from Greek salads to fried pickles, burgers, veggie tacos and Kale chips. You won't want to miss out on happy hour everyday from 3:00 pm to 6:00 pm and sample a Next Door Margarita made to please the taste buds. Just in front of the patio, visitors will have a fun view of an inground fountain and the constant flow of passengers making their way towards Amtrak and DIA bound trains. Sit back, relax and let the rhythm of downtown Denver be the backdrop to your delicious end-of-the-day treat.

Tap Fourteen Rooftop Beer Garden

1920 Blake Street, Denver, Colorado 80202

The Mile-High City motivates visitors to take a chance on a new and improved vantage point. When it comes to people watching, Tap Fourteen Rooftop Beer Garden does it right. With two stunning locations including downtown Denver overlooking Coors Field and an Uptown residence as well, the hardest decision will be deciding which venue proves right for you. The downtown property takes visitors up a few flights of stairs to the rooftop of Hayter's and Co. for a picturesque view and passion for all things craft beer. Nearly always bustling with newbies and patrons alike, Tap Fourteen is a high-energy scene that celebrates the best Denver offers when it comes to beer.

With views of crowds below, guests order at the rustic wooden bar and make their way to one of several benches scattered over the rooftop. In the hot summer months, expect an overhead mist to keep you cool as you sample all of Tap Fourteen's tasty drinks. While the menu features Colorado beef, it's the signature cocktails that keep patrons coming back for more. Don't forget to try the jalapeno margarita when you swing by this Colorado-made haven of taste and good times.

ViewHouse Ballpark

2015 Market Street, Denver, Colorado 80205

There's something about taste and a good view that makes a downtown Denver locale irresistible. ViewHouse Ballpark location is the perfect mix of fine-dining establishment, rooftop relaxation and game day getaway. In the heart of downtown Denver, this restaurant is extra spacious while delivering up cozy corners and impeccable views that make the experience most excellent and even intimate. Guests can choose to dine on the lower level interior while enjoying towering ceilings hoisted up by rustic brick walls. The ambiance is finished off with a large home-style bar complete with tv screens and team flags to set the scene.

Upstairs, it only gets better. A sprawling rooftop patio with vantage points looking out over downtown and Coors Field provides the ultimate pre-game party venue. With enough room to comfortably fit a large group or provide a great dinner for two with a breezy top table, ViewHouse is flexible, delicious and scenic. Come for a drink and stay for lunch or dinner. The menu includes tasty favorites from spinach and artichoke dip alongside lime-soaked tacos to Portobello sandwiches and hot-seared salmon just to name a few.

ACME Delicatessen

1701 Wynkoop Street at Union Station, Denver, Colorado 80202

Whether you're passing through while catching a train, or just in the mood for some thrilling people-watching, ACME Delicatessen is a great stop to satisfy hunger and social interest. Located directly in the station, ACME Delicatessen is an easy way to pick up something fresh with options for sitting back and enjoying the hustle and bustle of people on their way through. Open for breakfast, lunch and dinner, this cozy deli-style stop delivers up a great variety of bagels, sandwiches and salads made to order. From the Railroad Rueben to The Caprese, ACME Delicatessen is dedicated to convenience, taste and customer service.

Once you've got your delicious mid-day bite in hand, make your way over to one of the plush couches that are scattered throughout the station's main terminal. If those are occupied, you'll be pleased to find a number of casual wooden benches lining the walk ways recalling the glory days of train travel alongside studded booths that are reminiscent of worn luggage. While you're sure to be inspired by the variety of people passing before you, a look up is worth the glance as well. Towering chandeliers and a chic balcony hosting the primary floors of The Crawford Hotel meet the eye with all the beauty and labor of love dedicated during the station's massive renovation which was completed in 2014.

For a Night Out on the Town

Denver is full of options when it comes to exploring the city's flavorful stops, but when you're ready for a night out you'll want to head towards the neighborhoods with the food to fit the mood. Whether it's a first date, anniversary or night out with friends, here are a couple of locations that always deliver up the delicious with the added guarantee of an incredible atmosphere.

Avelina

1550 17th Street, Denver, Colorado 80202

Where great food, delicious drinks and top-notch hospitality collide, Avelina sets the pace when it comes to attentive service and overall amazing atmosphere in lower downtown Denver. Affectionately referred to as LoDo, this neighborhood is lively during the day and hosts an array of chic options for satisfying hunger when the sun goes down. Avelina is a comfortable and elegant option for dining with a spacious, open floor plan and large, soft lighting designs that maintains an intimate feel from early evening to well-beyond.

As perfectly appropriate for a romantic dinner for two as a group night out, the chic ambiance gives way to tasty meal options that include everything from duck liver mousse and Colorado striped Bass to artichoke salami flatbread and tender Ribeye steak. Those with dietary specifications will be pleased to find an extensive menu dedicated to gluten-free and Pescatarian dining options.

Morton's, The Steak House

1745 Wazee Street, Denver, Colorado 80202

Award winning steaks, delectable seafood options and a staff dedicated to creating long-lasting impressions, Morton's is an ideal dining establishment when you're looking for a classy locale that provides top-tier quality meats and a diverse menu. White clothed tables, shining chandeliers and music to set the mood, a night at Morton's will leave you with great vibes and a delicious feeling.

While you're there, take some time to appreciate an exemplary seafood selection including Maine Lobster Cocktail, baked Escargot or Tuna Tacos. Top of your visit by making the most of Morton's wine list which host over 200 find-wine options at each of their locations.

Izakaya Den

1487-A South Pearl Street, Denver, Colorado 80210

For the perfect blend of international flair and comfortable digs to dine with friends, Pearl Street provides the solution nearly every time. Charming, quaint and easily accessible, Pearl Street offers up a number of specialty restaurants that combine quality and casual atmospheres to make the most of a night out or a weekend of flavorful exploration. Izakaya Den at 1487 is a remarkable fusion of traditional Japanese fare with a kick of tapas on the side. Menu items are diverse and blend sushi, Izakaya specialties and international infusion. Unique in presentation, ambiance and taste, Izakaya Den is an exciting and exotic stop to tantalize the taste buds.

Feel free to explore the two open levels of Izakaya that are divided by exposed beams, sprawling glass windows and clean-lined seating arrangements. Gentle accents including mini waterfalls, ponds, foliage, bamboo and crisscrossed dividers complete with intricate lighting sconces set the scene. Overall, the restaurant layout allows for a private feel within the greater dining area. During the summer months, an open-air patio is available for seating and in the evening, glitters with bistro lights that keep the good times going well beyond sunset. Servers are extremely knowledgeable on the variety of menu items and are happy to help you pair up the perfect starter and main dish while complimenting this fun mix of flavors with the ideal wine or sake selection.

Que Bueno Suerte!

1518 South Pearl Street, Denver, Colorado 80210

When you're looking for bold Mexican flavors with a unique Denver twist, Que Bueno Suerte is your absolute best bet. Bright, fun and filled with flavor, this South Pearl Street gem is aesthetically pleasing and comes with a menu to match. As soon as you step in the door, you're met with an explosion of color and unique character. Bright red, semi-circle booths are perfect for intimate meetings while the bold central bar creates a cozy atmosphere for those looking to mingle. Giant, artful lighting in dazzling colors cover the ceiling while glass paneling and exposed beams add a modern flair.

When it comes to choosing something tasty, the options are both delicious and diverse. Chips and salsa paired with Queso Fundido are potential starters easily followed by Chile Relleno or Pollo con Mole. If you're looking to share, the chicken and cheese empanada is a must-try. With tacos plentiful and a Lavender Lemon Drop Martini chilled to perfection, everything available is worth trying at least once.

For Feeling Free

There are days that call for a completely casual approach to dining. From comfort food to food that just makes you feel free, here are a few stops to enjoy a day just for you. Your taste buds will thank you.

Backcountry Delicatessen

1617 Wazee Street, Denver, Colorado 80202

For many who originally hail from Colorado, spending time communing with the natural world is a way of life. Colorado offers up all the splendor of mountains, rugged landscapes and hiking trails heading towards each and every horizon. When it comes to taking on nature, food has a way of becoming a central theme for not only survival in the great outdoors but creating an experience full of flavor. What started as a provisions-style sandwich shop in Steamboat Springs in 1999 quickly grew into what it is today. With the heart and health of an outdoor adventurer in mind, Backcountry Delicatessen was born. Today, this delicious delicatessen has locations in Steamboat Springs as well as Fort Collins and Denver.

With a menu that's fresh and ingredients made to boost energy and endorphins when it's time to get outside, this quick and convenient deli-style stop makes ordering a delicious dish easy. Start your day with a breakfast sandwich or swing by over lunch for a specialty sandwich. Order by meat preference or go for a European-style Bavarian Club complete with applewood smoked bacon and dill pickles. With a variety of soups, salads and sides available, Backcountry Delicatessen gives guests an opportunity to create their dining experience, all within the comfort of a quaint location in the heart of downtown Denver.

The Wooden Table

2500 East Orchard Road, Greenwood Village, Colorado 80121

When it comes to comfort food, nothing quite beats a night full of fantastic Italian fare. For those moments you're craving a tasty locale that provides a charming atmosphere without the downtown hustle and bustle, The Wooden Table is a great fit. Located in the Denver suburb of Greenwood Village, this restaurant offers up an extensive Italian menu while providing a nice, neighborhood feel. Tucked within a larger square complete with clothing stores, bakeries and home goods, The Wooden Table maintains a sense of family with an outdoor patio, intimate indoor seating arrangements and soft lighting to keep it all cozy.

The Wooden Table uses fresh, local ingredients in all of their dishes and provides a menu that revolves with the season. Appetizers can include polenta, mussels and grilled flatbread while main course options put an Italian twist on pork, chicken and duck dishes. Pasta is always ready to be served and staff are extremely knowledgeable on fantastic wine pairings to bring out the best in your culinary selections.

Jax Fish House and Oyster Bar

1539 17th Street, Denver, Colorado 80202

When you're looking for a place to eat where you can just be you and have some fabulous seafood on the side,

Jax Fish House and Oyster Bar is everything you need. This laid-back locale is always bustling with patrons and visitors. Its Union Station adjacent address has kept the crowd flowing through the front doors since its opening in 1996. While the bar takes center stage in the setup, there's comfortable seating options everywhere you look as well as the option to eat outdoors.

The menu is made for seafood lovers and provides delicious bites with a home-cooked feel. With French onion oysters and calamari starting you off, you'll be tempted to follow it up with a crab, trout or salmon dish. Between the brick walls, you'll find an oasis of savory seafood flavors, all yours for the trying.

Cuba Cuba Sandwicheria

5322 DTC Boulevard, Greenwood Village, Colorado 80111

The Denver Tech Center is generally regarded as a business district on the southern outskirts of the city, but it's also a central hub for dining opportunities. One of the most fun and tasty stops when traveling through the Tech Center is Cuba Cuba Sandwicheria. Come in to eat, call for carry out or have it delivered right to your door. No matter what way you take it, this place undeniably brings the Latin flair and flavor.

Cuba Cuba brings the best of the authentic island to your sandwich, drink, wrap and plate order. Menu items like the Pan con Lechon and the Cubano are

26

made with Cuban breads and authentic Cuban meats. Together, they provide for a delicious combination that's hard to resist. For daytime stops make sure to complete your order with a rich coffee. For night time visits, don't miss out on the hand-crafted Cuban cocktails.

For Your Sweet Tooth

When your sweet tooth demands attention in Denver, you won't be lacking for options. While the city boasts a vast array of healthy dining establishments, it equally caters to the sugar-friendly folks that live here or are simply passing through. Take some time to indulge in a few of these yummy locales when it's time to feed the sugar craving.

Milk and Cake Yogurt & Cupcakes

6345 East Hampden Avenue, Denver, Colorado 80222

This unique sweets-combination shop is an incredible place to find both customized frozen yogurt options and cupcakes too! Drop by and browse the 16 self-serve frozen yogurt stations until your taste buds are satisfied. Small sample cups give you enough inspiration to create your next unique mix whether it's a standard chocolate and vanilla swirl or a more exotic peach, mano and fruity pebbles twist. When you're happy with your yogurt selections, make your way up the toppings bar to add a colorful mix of fresh fruits, candies and syrup to top it all off.

If you're more in the mood for cupcakes, Milk and Cake is a full-service bakery! Specializing in cupcakes of all shapes and sizes, you'll find a menu that provides everything from Lemon Poppyseed with Lavender frosting, to French Toast with a side of Maple Pecan. Brownies and specialty cakes are also options when it's your turn to order. Baked fresh daily, Milk and Cake is dedicated to providing mouth-watering cupcakes and cold frozen yogurt that will keep you coming back for more.

Protein Bar & Kitchen

1001 17th Street, Denver, Colorado 80202

Sugary goodness doesn't automatically come to mind when someone mentions Protein Bar, but it's their incredible smoothie selection that gives them a prime place on the sweet tooth list. While their menu offers up a variety of fresh and healthy options including Falafel bowels, salads, soups and wraps, their smoothies maintain the health factor while delivering big on sweet taste.

When you stop by, try an energizing protein-infused smoothie that delivers big flavor at the same time. Specialty drinks pop up during holidays and with the changing seasons, but all-time favorites continuously include the *Berry Good* which blends blueberry, strawberry, banana and vanilla. If you're looking for the caffeine kick, try a *Beauty Brew* blend or for something with a focus on Acai, order the *Joke A'Caid* made to satisfy with blueberry, vanilla and Acai berry.

Gateaux Bakery

1160 Speer Boulevard, Denver, Colorado 80204

Named Denver's best bakery by well-known publication *5280* the past eight years in a row, this Speer Boulevard bakery successfully dazzles customers with a vast array of sugary sweets made to taste daily. Fresh out of the oven, a stop at Gateaux is an experience in savory aromas as you're met with shining glass cases carefully displaying beautiful confections including torts, tarts, cakes and cookies to name a few. Renowned for their customized desserts and designs, Gateaux is ready and willing to create personalized cakes upon request for any and all important upcoming events. Stop by for a cookie and stay to browse an incredible selection of delicious desserts. Easy to find, just keep an eye out for the bold black and white awning to make your way towards this sugary stop.

For You Global Gastronomy Needs

With the influx of newcomers to Denver over the past several years has also come an upswing on the market of international cuisine. From Asian infusion to bold Mexican specialties, the possibilities are nearly endless when it comes to finding that tasty, exotic dish from afar you've been searching for.

Blue Sushi Sake Grill

1616 16th Street Mall, Denver, Colorado 80202

Chic, intriguing and full of delicious flavor, this sushi hub is a great downtown stop when you're seeking a lively atmosphere and a side of sake. The dim lighting and blue accent decor give the restaurant a trendy vibe, while the cuisine ranges from traditional sushi dishes to contemporary infusions. Feel free to order at the bar for a social experience or pick a table for a sit-down dinner. Take away options are available, but make sure you try a *Bluetini* blueberry-infused vodka specialty with a hint of lime before you go!

Rhein Haus

1415 Market Street, Denver, Colorado 80202

This Bavarian hub of beer, brats and beyond provides an authentic and fun taste of Germany right downtown. Hosting two levels of dining and entertainment there are options to cozy up to the sprawling wooden bar and order the best of German beer or settle down for a tasty and filling meal with family and friends. To keep the atmosphere lively, you'll find an area sectioned off on the second floor exclusively for games of Bocce Ball! Get the whole family involved, invite a first date or bring your team and see who's up to the challenge. The towering, exposed beam ceilings and wooden-detailed decor make this space truly feel like a Bavarian getaway. Make sure to try a giant pretzel, curry wurst or mini brats and wash your selection down with with a dark Warsteiner to make your taste of Germany a meal to remember.

Bistro Vendome Rendezvous Des Amis

1420 Larimer Street, Denver, Colorado 80202

When you don't quite have the time to make it to that left-bank café in Paris that you've been dreaming of, Bistro Vendome in downtown Denver will pick up the slack. A chic, tasteful locale offering up fine French cuisine with the ambiance to match, this bistro brings the flavor in full force. Nestled within the historic Sussex building Bistro Vendome has an incredible menu accompanied by a full-service bar. With plates brimming over with charcuterie, main dishes that include confit de canard and chocolate soufflé just a spoonful away, you'll come with France on the brain and leave satisfied. Don't forget to try the amazing assortment of cheese available at both brunch and dinner time visits.

For Feeling Nostalgic

Denver takes visitors directly into the urban heart of culture, history, art and so much more. Anytime you travel, there's a sense of wonder and thrill at the sheer number of new things you can potentially see in a single day. Sometimes, when the sightseeing is done, you just want a place you can kick back and feel like you're at home. When it comes to nostalgic comfort food, you might need to embrace your *academic* past to tastefully enjoy your traveling present.

Public School Restaurant and Bar

1959 16th Street, Denver, Colorado 80202

You read that right. Public School is downtown Denver's most throw-back themed restaurant and bar that has earned its status as a popular kids' hangout. Public School delivers up an all-American menu for the whole family that takes you back to the days of science, reading and arithmetic by using academic themes as interior decor schemes!

From globe-lined windows to menus that look like notebooks, this place is as charming as it is tasty. Serving brunch, lunch, dinner and happy hour specials, anytime you're hungry is a great time to head to Public School. With pizza, salads, burgers and sandwiches all on the menu, make sure you take the time to notice the fun wall-side extras that include chalk boards, science notes and some addition problem posters to keep you sharp while you wait for your food to arrive.

For When You're Feeling Fancy

There are times when a casual dinner will do, and other days when something requiring a more exclusive feel is called for. When you're in Denver and hoping to dine in style, give this downtown Italian treasure a try!

Osteria Marco

1453 Larimer Street, Denver, Colorado 80202

A visit to Osteria Marco is an experience in fine Italian dining right in the heart of Denver. While the name implies a casual place to meet with friends over great food, there is an artisanal spirit to the decor and menu that makes Osteria Marco a place that feels like a fanciful step up from a local hangout. It's the details that make this menu memorable and once you've ambled down the entrance stairs to the softly illuminated, brick-walled dining room below there's plenty to try. Once seated beneath the endless racks of wine bottles glimmering in the glow of table candles and tastefully hung curtains, you'll begin to scour the menu and want to try one of each.

Osteria Marco takes personalized Italian taste to the next level. With fresh-pulled Mozzarella delivered up daily alongside favorites such as Burrata, smoked Prosciutto and Gorgonzola Picante, your starter leads the way captivating the senses with bold flavors. With pizza, paninis and a string of Antipasti to choose from, it's hard not to let your imagination run wild at Osteria Marco. Whatever your selection, don't forget to ask your server about the extensive wine and specialty cocktail list.

Chapter 3: The Heart of Denver's History

Denver is a city that prides itself on a modern, forward-thinking approach to life. With a reputation for being ahead of the curve when it comes to making the controversial common-place, Denver is an open-thinking city with urban appeal. That being said, it all started somewhere. Looking back at some of those unique places that define old-Denver gives visitors a glimpse into just how far the city has come, and what it still treasures from long ago. Here's a look at a few places that have stood the test of time and managed to evolve in the heart of Denver as it's made its way into the modern age.

Union Station

1701 Wynkoop, Denver, Colorado 80202

The Lower Downtown Historic District of Denver is home to one of the city's most iconic and historic landmarks. Easy to recognize by the florescent sign hovering over the façade when the sun goes down, Union Station has been an easily identifiable site of significance in Denver for over 100 years. Complete restoration on Union Station was finally finished in 2014 after several years of hard work. The result is a hub of culture, convenience and transportation that has transformed a once dilapidated stop into the stunning center of commerce and intrigue it is today.

While Union Station is a functioning train station, it contains much more than that for the general public. If you are traveling from Union Station, you'll find easy access to both Amtrak and a city train that takes passengers to and from Denver International Airport. Within the walls of Union Station, a bustling world awaits. The grand renovation resulted in a space that is chic, functional and soaring. From high stone ceilings adorned with massive chandeliers and stone-detailed railings, to charming booths and benches carefully arranged upon shining floors, Union Station gives off more of a social club vibe. Giant windows on both sides of the building bring the downtown world in and allow for a fluid feeling to the movement of the crowds. If you stop around the holidays, it's thrilling to see the station covered in sparkling decor and a towering, decorated tree to complete the look.

While you're waiting for a train, or just stopping to admire the view and people watch too, there's plenty to keep you occupied. Union Station hosts a number of delicious and diverse restaurants and coffee stops. Snack kiosks keep the essentials at hand, while a souvenir shop satisfies those last-minute Denver-centric gifts on the list. If you're in the mood for a drink, Terminal Bar occupies a large portion of the floor and is a great place to unwind. The Crawford Hotel is built directly into Union Station, with rooms on the private second floor and is a great and convenient option if you're only stopping through for a short time. It's not uncommon to walk into Union Station and stumble upon a black-tie event being held in the foyer or wedding pictures in the works. With so much life, culture and aesthetic appeal, it's not hard to understand why it's become such a central point of social life in Denver.

Brown Palace Hotel & Spa

321 17th Street, Denver, Colorado 80202

1892 marked the grand opening of the Brown Palace Hotel & Spa in Denver and this fantastic location has continued to be a luxurious landmark in the city ever since. Big names have graced the halls of the Brown Palace Hotel and as the reputation for greatness grew, so did the list of visitors. Everyone from Charles Lindberg to Madeline Albright, Helen Keller to Robin Williams has made The Brown Palace Hotel their Denver home away from home. A slew of celebrities and stars including Taylor Swift, Snoop Dog and The Beatles have left their mark along the way as well. In fact, most U.S. Presidents have made The Brown Palace their landing pad at one point or another when visiting Denver. It's a legend and cultural point of identity for the city and that special status isn't lost on guests. This hotel provides a feeling of high-class living while maintaining that authentic Denver feeling with its modern downtown location.

Ownership continues to place a priority on sustainability by focusing on using reusable and recycled products. This is an important focal point as the hotel has 241 guest suites towering into the downtown skyline behind their brownstone façade. Rooms maintain their 19th century architectural design while providing modern appliances, luxurious linens and charming details that give guests a feeling of privilege. The spa offers everything from Swedish massage to hair care treatments. When you stay at the Brown Palace Hotel & Spa, you'll have access to decadent Champagne brunches, afternoon teas and delicious in-house dining experiences. Gold detailing, grand arches and towering ceilings are just a few of the spectacular views that greet you when you walk in. Whether you come to stay or just step in for a look around, The Brown Palace Hotel & Spa is a must-see when you're in the Denver area.

Red Rocks Amphitheatre

18300 W Alameda Parkway, Morrison, Colorado 80465

While the address technically places this rocky landmark in Morrison, many Denverites would happily claim Red Rocks Amphitheatre as their own. A short 30 to 40-minute drive from downtown Denver, Red Rocks Amphitheatre is a marvel and musical wonder to behold. With several levels of parking available on the dusty road leading up to Red Rocks, you'll want to get out and walk the last few bends if only for the view.

Red Rocks has long been the place to go when you want to hear great music in a scenic setting offering up great acoustics. With a sprawling stage built between natural rock formations sound smoothly glides through the semi-circle benches that pave the mountain-side floor from stage to top. Nearly every big name in music has made their way to Red Rocks at one point or another and tickets go quickly when the new seasonal lineup is released. If you stop by simply to admire, make sure to go through the museum whose entrance is clearly marked on the main path leading to the Amphitheatre. Inside, you'll find breathtaking mementos from guitars to jackets and much more signed by artists who have a close connection to this famous stage. Loved by musicians and nature-lovers alike, a trip to Red Rocks Amphitheater is a short trek worth making when you come to Denver.

The Daniels and Fisher Tower

1601 Arapahoe Street, Denver, Colorado 80202

Originally built in 1911 as a part of the infamous Daniels and Fisher Department Store, this iconic sky-scraping landmark rises into the air 372 feet and overlooks all of downtown Denver. Daniels and Fisher went out of business in the 1950's and by the early 1970's the dilapidated building was heading towards complete destruction. Community efforts to preserve the clock tower succeeded and what we have today is a beautiful venue to reflect on Denver's past and enjoy today's special occasions. With its Italian Renaissance façade neatly contrasted against Denver's downtown brick walled-hues, it's both intriguing to view and even more fun to visit. Guests can travel up to the 20th floor to enjoy a breathtaking view of the mountains and city skyline or even host an event behind the charming clock faces. This locale quickly books for corporate events, weddings and proposals. Make sure to take a peek up at night as the clock tower is lit up regularly as a shining beacon of Denver's past, present and future.

Molly Brown House Museum

1340 Pennsylvania Street, Denver, Colorado 80203

The 1970's was a major turning point in the world of architectural Denver. As the city began to experience an increasing population, there was a trend of destruction in the name of modernism. Beautiful buildings complete with charming details and fascinating history were being torn down at alarming rates. While Denver natives were excited to be moving forward in the name of progress, there was real concern that the city's history was being extinguished along with the buildings. In the name of conserving spaces that told important stories, Historic Denver, Inc. was founded and in 1970, the group began their diligent work of purchasing, restoring and conserving important properties.

The Molly Brown House Museum was one of these very properties salvaged and saved by the group and today, is an amazing tour destination when you're looking for a way to commune with the city's past in a progressive setting. Molly Brown was a survivor of the Titanic disaster who spent the majority of her remaining years dedicating time to philanthropy and educational programs. The home itself is a stunning Victorian originally built in the 1880's. With interior plumbing, heating and turn-of-the-century detailing, this home is a testament to eclectic and chic styling of the ages. Carved stones, beveled roofing and wrap-around porches welcome tour groups and school groups alike. Easy to identify by the large stone lions that guard the front door, the Molly Brown House Museum is a place that continues the celebration of Denver's historic identity as the city marches forward into a modern wave of new construction.

The Tattered Cover Bookstore

1628 16th Street, Denver, Colorado 80202

With the first opening of its doors happening in 1971, it might not seem that The Tattered Cover Bookstore qualifies as historic in terms of a turn-of-the-century timepiece. However, the longevity Tattered Cover has experienced since stemming from this monumental moment in Denver's history makes it a locale worth acknowledging and falling in love with.

The Tattered Cover identifies as a cozy Indie-bookstore complete with places to lounge and read, a café for picking up a tasty bite and an overall atmosphere that encompasses Denver's sense for both the rustic and modern. Stocked from floor to ceiling with books of all tastes and genres, The Tattered Cover is a quaint place to stop and get out from the hustle and bustle of downtown life, even if just for a while.

If you're looking to interact with authors while you're in the city, make sure to check out The Tattered Cover's extensive lineup. This bookstore is well-known for its high-profile live events and their list often includes more than 600 authors and illustrators on an annual basis. Whether it's for a coffee, a quick read or a leisurely look around, The Tattered Cover is an intriguing place to pass through. Today, the bookstore has multiple locations including downtown, Union

Station, Aspen Grove, Colfax Avenue and most recently opened a location in Highlands Ranch.

Chapter 4: Denver's Dance Scene

Denver is a city full of nature-enthusiasts, but those who live here know that there is a vibrant dance scene to be experience as well. When you're visiting Denver and feel the need to find the beat, check out a few of these locations where dance is the delicious main dish being served.

The Clocktower Cabaret

1601 Arapahoe Street, Denver, Colorado 80202

Snuggled into the Daniels and Fisher Clocktower, The Clocktower Cabaret is an exciting club that hosts live entertainment with an old-world feel. The line-up includes everything from Burlesque to circus acts, dance parties to musical performances. Divided into two levels, this venue allows you to enjoy a cocktail at the bar above the crowd and then make your way down to the dance floor when you're ready to jump into the fun! A glittering atmosphere complete with gold chandeliers, bistro-style tables and velvet-trimmed walls gives the sensation that you've stepped out of the real world and into a 1920's Speak Easy. Get your dance shoes on and make your way to The Clocktower Cabaret when you're in the Denver area for a night of glitz, glamor and dance.

Black Belt Salsa

3550 Federal Boulevard, Denver, Colorado

Black Belt Salsa is a central hub for Latin dance lovers looking for a place to let loose in Denver. Built upon the idea that a little instruction leads to a life-long passion for dance, beginners can show up at 3550 Federal Boulevard on a Tuesday night for a class and stay well into the evening for social dancing and a lot of fun! Black Belt Salsa offers a number of events throughout the year including holiday-themed dances and performances.

If you're looking for more of a long-term commitment, Black Belt is often searching for new apprentices to join their training program for instructors. From classes that hone your skills to a club-vibe dance night that follows directly after, this dance group delivers the fun and helps you build dance confidence along the way.

Hart's Dancewear

7703 Ralston Road, Arvada, Colorado 80002

A passion for dance doesn't come with an age or style requirement. When it comes to attire that matches your dance vibe, Hart's Dancewear in Old Town Arvada is the place to stop. This charming store comes complete with an extensive inventory of dance clothing and shoes. From ballroom to jazz, ballet and tap in between, the staff is dedicated to making sure you're ready for your next dance-based event in comfort and style. Once you've buckled up your next pair of dance floor favorites, make sure to give them a test run on the authentic dance floor the store hosts in the back room. It's a fun stop that leaves you feeling excited for your next performance, or big night out!

La Rumba

99 West 9th Avenue, Denver, Colorado 80204

La Rumba offers Denver dancers an electric Latin venue to visit when they are in the mood to Salsa the night away. If you're interested in making sure your steps are up to par the location offers classes at varying times based on ability seven nights a week. Four nights a week the club opens up to the general public in what inevitably becomes an exciting night of delicious drinks and dancing. Sultry and sophisticated, La Rumba implements a dress code to keep it classy. Make sure to regularly check the event calendar for special performances and concerts being held at this location.

Chapter 5: An Educational Point of View

Denver is a hub of culture, art, history and outdoor enthusiasm, but it's also an incredible place to pick when you're considering the world of higher education. The city plays an important role in hosting students from around the globe who come for the vibrant lifestyle, focus on nature and unsurpassed academic opportunities.

University of Denver Colorado: CU in the City

1201 Larimer Street, Denver, Colorado 80204

The University of Denver Colorado has the unique distinction of utilizing Downtown Denver as it's academic heartbeat. The university's primary campus thrives in the hustle and bustle of the city-center, allowing students to experience the urban pace while remaining only a drive away from the stunning mountains and natural surrounding world. Functioning under the motto *CU in the City*, the University of Denver Colorado prides itself on giving its students the unique opportunity to study and work directly in the pulse of progress within the capital of Colorado.

The university offers programs as diverse as their student population including Bachelor, Master, PhD and certificate programs to accommodate varying academic goals and professional plans. Programs range from Education and Arts and Media to Business and Architecture. Over 600 internships are awarded each academic year and many of the 90,000 alumni remain in Colorado after graduation, having fallen in love with all there is to see and do in this exciting state.

Metropolitan State University

890 Auraria Parkway, Denver, Colorado 80204

For students with their heart set on a downtown Denver experience without breaking the bank, Metropolitan State University is a top public university option. Seamlessly integrated into the downtown scene, the university hosts a population of students seeking bachelor's and master's degrees at a lower cost than many of the state's larger schools. Metropolitan State University prides itself on delivering opportunities for smaller class sizes that on average place 21 students to each professor.

There is a big focus on internship opportunities at MSU and students enjoy the city-scape when it comes to finding that interesting fit to help boost a future career in Colorado. Denver's music, architecture and thriving business scene give MSU students a head-start on delivering their best in the professional world. With programs ranging from Hospitality to Aerospace Sciences, MSU gives students a variety of academic paths to choose from all within the vibrant city limits of Denver.

Chapter 6: Making the Most of Mile High Museums

There is so much to be done outdoors when visiting Denver, but it's important to note that there is an exciting world within the vast number of museums the city hosts as well! From science to art, dinosaurs to the history of flight, Denver is a place that places a great importance on preserving and educating the public through thoughtful presentation. Here are a few museums you won't want to miss as you make your way through the Mile High City.

Denver Art Museum

100 W 14th Avenue Parkway, Denver, Colorado 80204

The Denver Art Museum is awe-inspiring from the moment you arrive at the front doors. This edgy, modern feat of architectures makes one think of a space ship carefully landing in the heart of Denver's Civic Center. The silvery façade leads visitors into a sprawling open-floor plan museum complete with easy-to-wander wings and over 70,000 works of art to explore.

The museum consistently hosts temporary exhibits that play upon pop culture as well as traditional works. Recent examples have included a Star Wars exhibit, a look at contemporary chairs through interior design and an exhibit highlighting women of

Impressionism. Permanent collections are equally as thrilling and cover everything from African art to European works, Native American art, photography and fashion. If you're traveling with kids, make sure to stop at the kids' zone where children have the opportunity to try their own hand at making a masterpiece. With so much to do and see, a trip to the Denver Art Museum will keep you coming back another day to make sure you've experienced every wing and piece of artwork to the fullest.

Denver Museum of Nature and Science

2001 Colorado Boulevard, Denver, Colorado 80205

Whether you're looking to experience the stars, take a walk with a T-rex or spend an afternoon thrilled by modern technology, The Denver Museum of Nature and Science is a great stop in Denver. This massive monument to the natural and scientific world around us is located directly next to the city zoo and comes complete with views of downtown and City Park.

The Denver Museum of Nature and Science gives visitors a daily opportunity to meander through exhibits that display natural world wonders with a focus on the body, prehistoric worlds, the limits of space and the beauty of gems and minerals. Make sure to stop by the discovery zone to give kids a hands-on scientific experience they won't forget. In addition to exhibit admission, you can buy tickets to the center's planetarium shows or spend an afternoon at the IMAX theater! When you're planning your visit, just be sure to arrive early especially if you're booking a stop for the weekend. The center is a fan favorite for locals and visitors alike and parking fills up fast sharing a lot with the zoo next door.

Wings Over the Rockies Air and Space Museum

7711 East Academy Boulevard, Denver, Colorado 80230

A great afternoon stop for visitors of all ages, the Denver Wings Over the Rockies Air and Space Museum is an old military plane hanger turned exhibition hall with tons to see and do. The hanger, which was a part of Lowry Airforce Base, was handed to a group of volunteers in 1994 with the mission creating a space dedicated to aviation education made for the public. For a small fee you walk into this open floor plan museum and begin with a short film featuring Harrison Ford as he delivers a bird's eye view over the Rockies from his personal plane and explains the thrill of aviation. From there, you can make your way around more than 182,000 square feet to marvel at iconic aircraft including bombers, carriers and passenger planes. With photo exhibits featuring famous airports and cockpit simulators to try out, there's an interactive portion to this museum that makes it unforgettable.

Once you've explored the skies, it's time to look a bit further and make your way through the space exhibit. A full space capsule lets visitors walk through what's it's like to live in space. Once you've seen Earth from above, feel free to check out the space suits and moon rocks that are on display. From videos to activities, revolving exhibits and the chance to peek inside a WWII cargo plane, this is a museum you won't want to miss.

Denver Botanic Gardens

1007 York Street, Denver, Colorado 80206

Just outside Denver where the mountains reach to the sky, it's easy to be awed by the natural beauty this city and state offer up. For those Denver days when you don't have the time to travel outside city limits, there's a place that brings the beauty of the natural world right to you. The Denver Botanic Gardens is a 24-acre oasis of natural wonders right in the heart of Denver. The Garden brings the best of the plant world to the urban center by creating a place where visitors can get an up-close look at stunning foliage from across the globe. With exhibits highlighting flowers that bloom throughout Colorado to acres dedicated to Asia, South Africa and beyond, this is a stop that's sure to please the senses and restore your peace of mind. Be sure to check out the water gardens that host a pyramid right in the middle of pristine water lilies and gently flowing ponds.

Denver Firefighters Museum

1326 Tremont Place, Denver, Colorado 80204

The Denver Firefighters Museum is yet another Denver landmark saved by groups of citizens dedicated to preserving the history of the city through architectural restoration and rejuvenation. This firehouse dates back to 1882 and when its usefulness was deemed lacking in 1978, a group called The Denver Fire Reserves began the process of transforming it into the museum it is today. Completed in the name of educating visitors on Denver's rich history of fighting fires, this is both an informative and interactive visit.

Entering the museum, you're met with an easy to follow path through the history of firefighting. From horse draw water apparatus to the high-tech equipment of today, a trip to this museum is a trip through time. The museum highlights major city fires with a focus on the individuals who risked their lives for others. Children can suit up in play gear and get imaginative as they climb on a stationary fire truck in the main hall. Guests are invited to make their way up to the second floor and get a close-up look at what life in the firehouse was like for firefighters. There, you'll find reconstructions of bedrooms, clothing and equipment, showing what it really took to be ready to handle an emergency at all hours of the day or night.

Chapter 7: Journey Just Outside Denver

Denver is full of exciting places to see, experience and explore, but what's even more thrilling is the fact that just beyond the Denver city limits more excitement awaits. Traveling mere miles in any given direction from downtown opens up a world of potential and it's easy to fit these side-trips into your Denver-bound itinerary. Here are a few places to consider when you're looking to make the most of Denver and just beyond.

Edelweiss

34 East Ramona Avenue, Colorado Springs, Colorado 80906

When you're craving some hearty German cuisine, Edelweiss in Colorado Springs is worth the drive. Pleasing the palate of those who love European fare for over 50 years, Edelweiss brings the flavor alongside the authentic ambiance. Tucked away on Ramona Avenue, look for the decorative sign as you make your way up the street. The exterior is easily identifiable with rustic rock columns and a cozy red-lined rooftop making one think of a Bavarian village.

Guests can choose to sit inside amongst floor to ceiling German apparel and trinkets including woodland scenes, antlers and old cottage paintings. If you drop by during the colder months, you'll be pleased to settle in next to one of three warm fireplaces. If you've come for the extensive German beer list, you'll want to make your way out to the *Biergarten* patio where you can enjoy a lager under twinkling lights and shady umbrellas. Make sure to indulge in all the Schnitzel, Sauerbraten and Bratwurst you'd like for a true taste of Germany while in Colorado Springs. The baked Brie and Flammkuchen come highly recommended as starters!

Cheyanne Mountain Zoo

4250 Cheyanne Mountain Zoo Road, Colorado Springs, Colorado 80906

Far from your average day at the zoo, a visit to Cheyanne Mountain Zoo takes you up 6,800 feet in elevation to the most open-air zoo experience you'll find in the United States. Built directly into the mountainside, Cheyanne Mountain Zoo provides breathtaking opportunities to not only interact with animals but do it all in a setting that provides unsurpassed views of the city below. Guests wander looping trails taking them past exquisite exhibits with space for animals to roam that goes far beyond traditional zoo setups.

Feel free to make your way up the rustic, wooden stairs connecting many levels of the zoo and providing new vantage points for viewing. Visitors will be introduced to over 30 endangered species during their visit with opportunities to hand-fee giraffes along the way. Commemorate your Cheyanne Mountain Zoo visit with a trip to the gift shop before you go, and then make your way down the gorgeous winding road that leads back to downtown Colorado Springs.

The Rocky Mountain Dinosaur Resource Center

201 S Fairview Street, Woodland Park, Colorado 80863

The state of Colorado has long been a place where Paleontologists continue to discover hidden gems in the form of dinosaur fossils right below the surface. As a way to educate, inform and display some of the most incredible finds, The Rocky Mountain Dinosaur Resources Center was created. Easy to find with Palm Trees and a dinosaur replica waiting right outside the front door, visitors are met with an impressive collection of standing fossils arranged to display these prehistoric creatures' immense stature and stunning forms. Exploring exhibits that feature both dinosaurs and marine reptiles, the Rocky Mountain Dinosaur Resource Center is a great place to bring the whole family when you're looking for a place that brings prehistoric history to life right before your eyes.

Pueblo Riverwalk

101 S Union Avenue, Pueblo, Colorado 81003

If you travel southeast approximately 40 minutes from Colorado Springs you'll stumble upon Pueblo, Colorado. This city is worth visiting for the Riverwalk alone. When you're looking for a peaceful place to wander riverside, Pueblo offers up scenic views with great dining opportunities as well. Excursion boats are available if you feel like leisurely floating down the 1-mile channel. If you're more in the mood for walking, make your way alongside the smooth, easy to meander path and you'll be pleased to occasionally find yourself in the middle of a mid-day Farmer's Market or other seasonal street festival.

Rocky Mountain National Park

1000 US Hwy 36, Estes Park, Colorado 80517

Colorado calls to those who love the mountains and no place quite says Colorado like Rocky Mountain National Park. Just an hour and a half drive northwest from Denver, this national park brings everything an outdoor enthusiast could want. With opportunities for camping, hiking, viewing wildlife and connecting with nature, a visit to Rocky Mountain National Park isn't one you'll soon forget. Guests are free to explore the more than 415 square miles the protected park encompasses. Within that area visitors will discover nearly 300 miles of hiking trails. A trip through Rocky Mountain National Park brings you in touch with free roaming animals, incredible wild flowers and summit views unlike any other. Reservations can be made for those looking to camp throughout their visit and a trip to Rocky Mountain National Park wouldn't be complete without a journey up Trail Ridge Road. At an elevation of 12,000 feet, the Alpine horizon is limitless.

Chapter 8: Parks for One and All

Visiting a park is a simple way to unwind and find some time for reflection, play and relaxation when you're in any city. When you're traveling through Denver, visitors will be pleased to find the city puts a great emphasis on creating and maintaining green spaces for the general public. Whether you're traveling with kids who crave a little playground time, or you're a solo traveler looking for a quiet place to call your own for just a while, there are several parks worthy of being put on your to-visit list. Here are just a few worth mentioning.

City Park

2001 Colorado Boulevard, Denver, Colorado 80205

Living up to its name, City Park is Denver's premier place to go when you're looking for a gorgeous green space right in the middle of the city. City Park is a unique area in that it houses the Denver Zoo as well as the Denver Museum of Nature and Science along with all the outdoor attractions one could crave in a city-center park. Established in the late 1800's, City Park continues to thrive as an area for social gatherings, an afternoon out with the kids or a getaway when the hustle and bustle of the city gets to be a bit much. Full of visitor-friendly lawns for sprawling out for a nap or enjoying a picnic, you can just as easily lounge here as jump into a friendly game of soccer.

Kids will love the sprawling wooden playground and when you're tired of the swings and monkey bars, make your way along the paved paths and admire the several ponds complete with ducks. If you're looking for an afternoon of exercise, many yoga classes regularly host sessions outdoors at City Park. A large central fountain provides a pristine place to stop and admire the view when you drop by for a visit. Surrounded by greenery but located directly in the center of Denver's thriving metropolis, City Park is a great place to explore. The only factor to take into consideration is parking. With its proximity to the zoo and science center, it can be tricky to find a place if you come on a weekend. Get comfortable with the idea of walking a little way to make it to the main entrance or consider taking the bus for this particular excursion.

Wallace Park

8501 E. Belleview Avenue, Denver, Colorado 80237

George M. Wallace Park is a surprising green find in the middle of Denver's Tech Center. Surrounded by residential neighborhoods and skyward reaching office buildings, this park is the perfect stop when you're looking for an easy-to-manage mid-day getaway. Looped by the Goldsmith Gulch Trail, runners and leisurely walkers will enjoy the 1.85 miles of smooth path through sprawling green fields and gentle hills and slopes.

If you come with the kids, be sure to stop at the mid-sized playground for some fresh-air adventures on the slides and swings. From here, make your way either direction on the loop for opportunities to skip blocks over the small stream of water that makes its way through the park. Various sizes of cement blocks create a fun maze of water-hopping fun when you're visiting Wallace Park. If you feel that you're due for a mid-day workout, try one of two areas designated for park-time exercise. These machines come complete with instructions for making the most of your outdoor regime and come with circuit recommendations to maximize muscle.

Cherry Creek State Park

4201 S Parker Road, Aurora, Colorado 80014

This 880-acre, mountain encompassed reservoir is an incredible add to your itinerary for a day immersed in the natural world. Season passes are available to enter the state park but if you're looking for a day excursion the entrance fee is $9.00 per vehicle and well-worth the price. Once inside, there are several stopping points that can be explored by car, on foot or by bike. Hiking trails, water-side alcoves and sprawling prairie make for an incredible view no matter where you set up for the day.

Cherry Creek State Park offers guests opportunities to make the most of water activities including boating, paddle boarding and designated swimming areas. Those who love to picnic will find expansive areas full of tables designed to enhance a perfect and delicious afternoon. When you're traveling with kids, make your way towards the beach playground where you'll find the best in sand, slides and waterfront wonders. Whether you're here to enjoy the water, the sand or the scenery, be sure to keep your eyes open for wildlife along the way. Several informational boards at each alcove inform visitors of the vast marine life that live within the park.

Commons Park

2101 15th Street, Denver, Colorado 80202

The Mile High City makes the most of the natural world by incorporating green space into urban Denver whenever the chance presents itself. One such place worth making your ways towards is Commons Park. Often used during the academic school year as a field trip destination, this park is a great place to spend an afternoon, observe wildlife and learn about the foliage that thrives in Colorado. Considered a gateway park to the South Platte River, those who love getting outdoors can take advantage of the many waterfront locales for relaxing and enjoying the view. An interesting mix of vantage points, Commons Park allows visitors the opportunity to enjoy towering skyscrapers alongside riverfront paths. It's urban fusion at its best and a sprawling testament to Denver's dedication to making sure the city remains a place where the natural and cityscape collide.

Water World

8801 N Pecos Street, Federal Heights, Colorado, 80260

While not a park in the traditional sense, since it's opening in 1979, Water World has continued to hold onto its status as Denver's favorite water park. Just 10-miles south of downtown Denver, this massive, watery wonderland is fun for the whole family and worth visiting when you're in the Denver area during the summer months. Proudly hosting the first two waterslides known to Denver, today the park has expanded to include everything from wave pools to tubing, high-speed slides to splash pools for little ones. Warming pools, plunge tanks and Gondola ride experiences make Water World a must-try if you're a visitor who loves to take a dive in the deep end. Cabana and bungalow rentals alongside on-site dining make a trip to Water World a comprehensive and convenient stop.

Ruby Hill Park

1200 W Florida Avenue, Denver, Colorado 80223

When the winter months roll around, those looking for snowy fun in Denver don't have to go far. Ruby Hill Park is an amazing option to satisfy those sledding and snowboarding cravings without having to head towards the mountains. Several slopes provide the perfect setting for taking the toboggan out for the day or trying your skills in the area designated for snowboards. Kids will enjoy the adjacent playground when they're tired of trekking back up the hills. From the top-most points of this park, you'll witness beautiful views and it's always a thrilling ride to the bottom. As of 2016, the park also hosts a 7.5-acre bike park complete with dirt jumps, slopes and skills course. With the addition of the bike park, Ruby Hill solidifies its place as a great place to visit no matter the season.

Chapter 9: Exclusively for the Kids

The diversity of activities and dining to be found in Denver makes it an amazing place to travel with kids. Whether you're traveling with picky eaters, short attention spans or those who need diversion that's dramatic and ever-changing, the incredible landscape and plethora of urban excitement makes for a setting suited to little ones and adults alike. Here are a few stops that are sure to get your kids excited about their next Denver adventure.

The Denver Zoo

2300 Steele Street, Denver, Colorado 80205

Located within the perimeters of City Park, the Denver Zoo is an 80-acre oasis of wildlife fun and adventure! Opening its doors for the first time in 1896, the zoo continues to be one of the most popular attractions in the Denver area. With so many wild animals to see and interactive things to do, it's not hard to see why so many people make their way this direction when they're visiting the city. Open year-round, the zoo provides a chance to explore a vast selection of exhibits that highlight local and exotic creatures.

When you're looking for an easy way to see the entire zoo, take a trip on the zoo train and stop for a carousel ride when you've reached the end of the line. Feedings and interactive presentations are brought to guests on a daily basis as you have close encounters with bears, birds, elephants, giraffes and so much more! Hungry after your zoo excursion? Make time to dine at Kamala Café which offers up bold flavors of the East. If you've forgotten one of those essential items like a water bottle or hat for a sunny day at the zoo, Safari Outfitters provides a convenient one-stop-shop for picking up what you need to make your day stress-free and fun.

Children's Museum of Denver

2121 Children's Museum Drive, Denver, Colorado 80211

Nestled along the boundaries of downtown Denver, the Children's Museum is a fun stop for kids of all ages looking to get rid of some extra energy and connect with their creative sides. With over 20 exhibits, two levels and 9-acres of green space complete with playgrounds, this is a haven of kid-like fun and entertainment where kids are free to be crazy and create something cool! With stops that give kids a chance to explore the details behind bubbles, energy, water and art there's bound to be something every child in your family loves. Kids will love painting a statue, creating bubbles as big as they are or taking a turn on the rock climbing and exploration maze! Educational and highly interactive, there's never a dull moment when you take time to visit the Children's Museum of Denver.

Monster Mini Golf

8227 S Holly Street, Centennial, Colorado 80122

While Monster Mini Golf is specifically geared towards the kids, adults will find it just as thrilling. A stop at this venue is an experience in monster-themed glow-in-the-dark mini golf! Illuminating and exciting, this is an activity made for all skill levels and a fun walk on the side of fantasy. From clown heads to fantastic beasts walking across the miniature greens, there's a scare in the air around every corner. Once you've completed the course, make your way towards the arcade for hours of follow up fun trying your hand at acquiring carnival-style prizes and playing video games. It's a virtual getaway complete with monster-esque memories perfect for the whole family.

AMF Monaco Lanes

6767 Leetsdale Drive, Denver, Colorado 80224

When all that sightseeing has you looking for a place where the kids can play, and the adults can enjoy a beverage, a stop at AMF Monaco Lanes is your best bet solution. This sprawling establishment comes complete with 40 lanes for making the most of your skills. Adults can easily supervise from the on-site sports bar while the kids count up the strikes. For those needing a bit more diversity, take a trip through the interactive arcade to make the most of your AMF Monaco Lanes day. Bowling here is built for both beginners and those who have earned legendary status on the lanes. The knowledgeable staff is happy to help make sure you're in the right shoes and using the correct weight ball before you start up.

Jumpstreet

10081 W Bowles Avenue, Littleton, Colorado 80127

When you're in Denver with the little ones and the energy level is through the roof, Jumpstreet provides the ultimate solution for getting rid of the wiggles. Hosting three locations between Littleton, Greenwood Village and Lakewood, this is a place that's convenient to find and worth the effort when young travelers need a place to let it all out. Built to match a child's imagination, each Jumpstreet location is divided into zones by age group to keep the fun safe and sound. Smaller children will enjoy a maze of easy-to-use bouncy houses and miniature trampolines where parents can supervise jump time. Older children can wander or run throughout the building at will, discovering and exploring an endless opportunity of activity centers.

Pay by the hour and let the kids run wild! They'll have an incredible time jumping on the full floor trampolines, making their way through an intricate bouncy house maze, swinging like Tarzan into the foam block pit or playing laser tag with new friends. Locations include a small cafeteria for purchasing snacks and beverages as kids inevitably build up an appetite. Parents can rest easy supervising from the comfort of a massage chair if the moment calls for it.

Whatever age group your little ones fall into, Jumpstreet is just the right place.

Cave of the Winds

100 Cave of the Wind Road, Manitou Springs, Colorado 80829

While it's a bit out of the way, a visit to Cave of the Winds is worth the drive and a magical place for kids to visit when you're in Colorado. An intricate network of caves in the Pikes Peak region of the state, Cave of the Winds was discovered by explorers in 1881 and today remains an unforgettable destination for exploration. A renowned stop for making family memories there are several tour options available depending on what your children are interested in.

If you're looking for a tour that everyone can enjoy together, consider booking the Discovery Tour. A knowledgeable guide will show you the way through several cave chambers and point out incredible rock formations along the way. A lantern tour gives you the option of exploring by candlelight. Families who thrive on adrenaline may enjoy the 2.5-hour trek through underdeveloped portions of the cave led by a guide through winding paths that require crawling and climbing. Beyond the caves, visitors will be thrilled to find a Wind Walker Challenge course, testing the limits of balance and bravery high above the ground. Thrill seekers will not want to miss a trip down the zip line while those looking for an otherworldly experience can take a turn in the virtual reality theater!

Union Station Fountains

1701 Wynkoop, Denver, Colorado 80202

The summer temperatures in Denver have a way of catching some visitors by surprise. Known for weather that fluctuates in interesting ways, a mid-summer trip might be an experience in mild weather one day, and triple digits the next. If you're in the city and find yourself needing a place to take the kids to cool off, make a stop at the Union Station Fountains. This easy to access area takes up about a block just to the left of the Union Station façade.

Right in the heart of downtown action, kids can take advantage of this urban watering hole! Multiple in-ground spouts line the sidewalk and make for a fun and entertaining sprinkler-type party. With plenty of benches close by and restaurants lining the station itself, parents can keep a close eye as children run, jump and play in the fascinating fountains that move to their own rhyme and rhythm.

Downtown Aquarium

700 Water Street, Denver, Colorado 80211

A great place to spend an afternoon with the kids no matter what season brings you to Denver is the Downtown Aquarium. Located just on the outskirts of the heavier hustle and bustle of central Denver, this aquarium brings just the right amount of interactive exhibits, fun marine life encounters and time spent exploring. An hour and a half is about the amount of time needed to fully experience this stop, which is perfect for just about any age group you may be traveling with.

A floor to ceiling window façade makes this venue easy to spot. Once inside, get ready to take a fun water-front picture available for purchase after you're through exploring. An escalator takes you upstairs to where the adventures starts. A clearly defined path through the aquarium leads you through exhibits featuring over 500 species of animals from across the planet. This aquarium is unique in that it hosts an exhibit featuring a mock flood zone to show the natural wear of water on ecosystems.

You might be surprised to stumble upon the aquarium's live-in tiger towards the end of your visit, complete with a viewing platform via hanging bridge. When all is said and done, make your way to the lower-level restaurant for an underwater dining experience. Every table provides a view of the full-length, 50,000-gallon accommodating aquarium. Showing up at just the right time gives you a front-row seat to the mermaid show where magic and underwater life collide.

Elitch Gardens

2000 Elitch Circle, Denver, Colorado 80204

Make sure the whole family gets to experience Elitch Gardens when you make your way to Denver. The city's most prized amusement park possession, this central hub of themed fun and entertainment can be found in the heart of downtown, making it a super unique stop. With a combination of thrill rides, age appropriate activities for little ones and water rides included, this is a downtown destination that's sure to bring some smiles.

Elitch Gardens regularly hosts concerts as well as special events which are fun if you're in the area at the time. You might also enjoy taking a trip down memory lane and attending one of the water park's drive-in movie night events! During the summer months, this is an option nightly beginning at approximately 7:30 pm. Even better...tickets are included with the price of admission! With so much to do at Elitch Gardens, you're definitely going to want to set aside an entire day for this kid-friendly excursion.

The Wild Animal Sanctuary

2999 Co Road 53, Keenesburg, Colorado 80643

The world over, the luscious landscape of Colorado is known for hosting some of the globe's most wonderous wildlife imaginable. Hiking through the forest or making your way up a mountainside, it's not uncommon to run into captivating creatures including bears, mountain lions and mountain goats. Powerful, majestic and equally intimidating, these creatures can remind us of just how diverse nature's line up really is.

So, what happens when those same animals find themselves in harms way at the hands of their human counterparts? It's hard to imagine beasts of such powerful stature needing assistance, but the professionals at The Wild Animal Sanctuary tell a very different side to the animal and human story.

Operating on more than 10,000 acres on two sites, The Wild Animal Sanctuary is a refuge for wild animals who have suffered at the hands of humans. Dedicated to creating a space that nearly perfectly imitates their natural environment, the professionals who work at The Wild Animal Sanctuary spend their days to keeping large animal welfare a top priority. While the facility hosts many of Colorado's own creatures including bears and mountain lions, the list of protected animals goes well beyond the state's boarders. Everyone from tigers to lions and wolves have sprawling space to recover and living fulfilling lives amongst their own kind.

Upon arrival, guests check in at the visitor center to take part in an official sign in process. The sanctuary runs primarily on donation and guests can give as they see fit to help the mission of the Wild Animal Sanctuary continue on well beyond the day of their visit. Once that's done, guest make their way towards the elevated walkways that wind through the sanctuary lands for observation. As a way of avoiding emotional stress that is caused when animals and people are separated at eye-level by glass enclosures this elevated pathway creates a seamless separation allowing guests to observe animals in a natural way that doesn't interfere with their routines or recovery. The pathway provides 1.5 miles of accessible walking path that leads through all the enclosures and open spaces.

At the end of the visit, guests can enjoy an ice cream at the central pavilion and reflect on what they've seen and learned. Far from a standard day's getaway, The Wild Animal Sanctuary is in the business of providing great chance in the name of animal conservation and protection. Visitors who donate can feel good knowing they've contributed to the well-being of some of the world's most spectacular creatures without affecting them in their habitats. It's a day that's sure to make a long-lasting impression!

Chapter 10: Top-Notch Shopping Stops

Known for its diverse art scene, lively adoration for hosting some of the best music festivals in the state and all-around engaging atmosphere, Denver is also a great place to come when you're in the mood to hit up some top-notch shopping venues. Whether you're looking for a place with all the right souvenirs, or an area dedicated to boutique clothing lines, there's something in the Mile High City for you.

16th Street Mall

1001 16th Street Mall, Denver, Colorado 80265

This pristine pedestrian promenade in the center of downtown Denver is a lively place where shopping, dining and entertainment collide. The block-long zone was built in dedication to the savvy shopper in all of us. If you're looking for an incredible place to grab a bite, get a drink and then get to some serious shopping, try any one of the 42 cafés that line the 16th Street Mall.

Once that's done you'll want to head towards Denver Pavilion where you'll find mall-style stores just waiting to be discovered. Don't feel like walking? Not a problem as the MallRide bus system provides easy to board, free transportation servicing the 16th Street Mall exclusively. Keep your eyes open if you visit in the evening hours as horse-drawn carriages tend to transform into the transportation mode of choice. For those that have visited Denver in the past, 16th Street Mall is worth a second visit. The recent population increase in the city encouraged local officials to invest in this area as a cultural point of attraction. With renovation and new laws in place to discourage loitering, the 16th Street Mall has quickly become an exciting, upbeat stop in the city where consumers come to make the most of their Denver getaway in style.

Larimer Square

Larimer Street, Denver, Colorado 80202

Every great city must start somewhere, and Denver is no exception to the rule. Considered the very first block in the city of Denver, this stretch of street is lovingly referred to as Larimer Square and today is a central hub of downtown communing and commerce. While the dining options are incredible, shoppers will love that they can easily stroll down Larimer Square and stumble upon big name brands right alongside Denver-specific styles. Stores like Aillea provide customers with top-line clean beauty products with a purpose beyond the colors. Cry Baby Ranch brings the western flair apparel to the area's vast selection while Element has everything you could dream you'd need for home furnishings. Not even the dogs are excluded from this shopping trip. Dog Savvy Boutique is the place to find exquisite accessories for your four-legged friend or have them treated to a puppy spa-day while you're out and about. Shops dedicated to hats, shoes and hiking gear will keep you busy as you take a walk down one of Denver's oldest paths remembering where the city started and enjoying what it is today.

Park Meadows Mall

8401 Park Meadows Center Drive, Lone Tree Colorado, 80124

This well-known Lone Tree locale is easily accessible when you're traveling through Denver and is a great place to go when you're looking for a traditional shopping stop with vast selections. Two levels complete with exposed beam ceilings and accessible escalators, this mall is unique it's ability to balance Colorado rustic décor with the all-American shopping experience. Make your way through big-name brands such as Aldo, American Eagle or Anthropologie while noticing the charming details along the way. Stonework reminiscent of a nature trail sets the scene for the penny toss pond complete with an indoor waterfall right in the center of Park Meadows Mall. Kids will love the chance to explore the Build-A-Bear Workshop or The American Girl Store. Keep in mind when you're traveling around the holidays that Park Meadows Mall is one of the city's finest places when it comes to meeting Santa in his element. Every year, the mall goes to extraordinary lengths to create a winter wonderland right within its own walls made to enchant visitors of all ages. Come to share your wishes with the North Pole's greatest celebrity himself and stay for the photos and elf-tastic craft stations. If a Santa stop is in the plan, make sure to arrive early as locals love Park Meadows winter time creations and before long, the line is guaranteed to be wound around the lower level.

When shopping has finally lost its shine, make your way to the upper level food court for a variety of dining selections. There's no shortage of options no matter what you prefer to munch in the middle of the day with locales like Panda Express, Subway and McDonalds readily available. If you're looking for more relaxed sit-down options, Park Meadows Mall hosts The Cheesecake Factory, Seasons 52 and The White Chocolate Grill. Just outside the front doors of the main entrance visitors will find a pathway leading to several separate store fronts and dining establishments that aren't physically connected to the main mall but are still a part of the Park Meadows family. Complete with a small bridge that spans a gentle man-made creek, a walk through this outdoor area of the mall is refreshing and great for enjoying an afternoon or evening in Lone Tree.

Historic Downtown Littleton

Main Street, Littleton, Colorado 80160

Sitting just outside of Denver is an historic gem perfect for the traveling shopper who enjoys a relaxed atmosphere and stores offering up specialty wares and souvenirs. Downtown Littleton thrives around a charming Main Street with many small, local businesses offering products such as trendy clothing lines, antiques and art. Carefully arranged alongside several cafés offering outdoor seating, Downtown Littleton is a great way to spend an afternoon when you're looking for a relaxed way to find those one of a kind purchases.

Ikea

9800 E Ikea Way, Centennial, Colorado 80112

This Swedish haven of ready-to-build home furnishings clearly isn't exclusive to Denver, but for those traveling in from out of town who don't have an Ikea nearby, it's an exciting stop to make! Massive in size but convenient in-home décor and planning, Ikea is easily identified from a distance by the sprawling yellow and blue storefront. You'll make your way up several sets of escalators at this location before entering the official showroom. Wander along the easily marked path as you make your way through demonstration living rooms, bedrooms, kitchens, patios and more.

The idea is to gather your inspiration and take down numbers of furniture pieces you fall in love with during your tour. Once you reach the warehouse, you'll have an opportunity to pick up an easy-to-roll cart and make your way to the appropriate shelving units to find those must-have items to take to check out. While large ready-to-build items like beds and dressers are always available, it's hard to pass through the utensil and home accessories section without picking up a potted plant, coaster set or other unique item that seems to just fit that hard to decorate corner of the house.

Ikea also has sections dedicated exclusively to home lighting and kid-friendly décor! A large variety of lamp sizes and shapes gives you the option of mixing and matching stands and shades to create a lighting style that's all your own. When it comes to putting those finishing touches on a child's room, bunkbeds, miniature play castles and organizational bins for those runaway toys come in bulk. Not sure how to put everything together just right? The staff at Ikea are trained to help you plan out your rooms or entire home. Swing by one of the kiosks and speak with a staff member about your particular layout and vision for home renovation.

If a trip to Ikea has left you famished when all is said and done, the store has got that covered too. Ikea hosts a full Swedish specialty café and provides a grab-and-go style market that you'll pass just on your way out the doors. Impossible to miss, the exit to Ikea smells like freshly baked cinnamon rolls more often than not. While they may be specialists in small quarter living decor, they tend to be masters when it comes to big Swedish flavor and the results are hard to deny. The professionals at Ikea have made an impressive mark on the city of Denver in very Swedish style.

Chapter 11: Hotels You Have to See to Believe

It's easy to book a vacation rental when you're headed towards Denver. It's even easier to find a cozy apartment share downtown close to all the action. With a market saturated with potential properties just waiting to be selected it may seem counter intuitive to go with a traditional hotel...until you see what Denver has to offer. A far cry from that Hilton Garden Inn you have in your mind, Denver is full of historic gems that come in the form of well-preserved hotels. Chic, conveniently located and full of rich stories, there are a few hotels in the Mile High City that are worth the reservation.

The Oxford Hotel

1600 17th Street, Denver, Colorado 80202

A well-loved icon of downtown, Denver The Oxford Hotel is easily recognizable with its charming brick façade and top-hatted doorman that stand outside to both greet and assist guests with luggage. The Oxford provides a room and so much more when you book a stay at this location. An integral part of the city since 1891, the hotel also houses the Cruise Room Bar and a full-service spa for guest to enjoy. When dinner time rolls around, Urban Farmer Steakhouse is the ultimate option as it is attached directly to the hotel.

The interior design of the hotel is as admirable as the rooming options. Art Deco details adorn nearly every wall and staircase. From rustic paneling to antique murals, there's hardly a place you can look where old-world comfort and charm aren't present. Even the room keys speak to days past with guests using large brass keys to enter their rooms and that must be returned to the front desk whenever one ventures out. Feel free to enjoy the colorful bird cage complete with feathered friends that sits at the reception desk. In the event you can't quite get a grasp on your vacation timeline, the elevator mats change to reflect the day of the week and are a fun extra when you're taking luggage upstairs.

Winding hallways and wood-railed staircases guide the way towards the many rooms available. Hallways are dotted with antique furniture and photos to match the time period the hotel was constructed. Once inside, guests will be pleased to find ultra-plush beds, dramatic turn of the century curtains and bathrooms that come complete with black and white checkered tiling straight out of the 1920's. If you're lucky enough to get a street view room, large floor to ceiling windows give a great vantage point on the excitement below.

If you come to Denver during the holidays, a stop into the lobby of The Oxford is a must-do as the hotel staff goes to extreme lengths to decorate for the season. Twinkling lights, beautiful bulbs and an 18-foot tree make for a stunning photo opportunity. If you are just dropping by for a look, don't be surprised to see other groups of visitors dropping by to do exactly the same thing. The Oxford has the reputation of being one of Denver's most haunted destinations and paranormal enthusiasts can't resist coming in to see for themselves.

The Crawford Hotel

1701 Wynkoop Street, Denver, Colorado 80202

Possibly one of the most luxurious choices when it comes to staying in downtown Denver, The Crawford Hotel comes with the added bonus of being located directly within Union Station! Guests will find the reception desk located conveniently on the ground floor of the main building and attendants will point the way to elevators hoisting you up to the second floor where rooms are located behind an entrance requiring a room key. Chic accommodations with all the best in modern amenities provide a fun place to getaway from it all while staying right in the heart of the action.

If you're looking to leave the hotel room for a while, make your way to the second- floor portion of Terminal Bar which provides a bird's eye vantage point on the hustle and bustle below as you sip your cocktail. When you're down, schedule a pick up with reception and make your way to one of Denver's downtown shows by way of a chauffeured Tesla! Free of charge, this service will leave you feeling like royalty as you make your way through the city in style.

Magnolia Hotel

818 17th Street, Denver, Colorado 80202

In true Denver style, the Magnolia Hotel is a downtown testament to preserving history with a modern twist. For those who appreciate a story that comes with renovated style, The Magnolia Hotel is the ultimate experience destination. Originally built in Denver in 1910, the hotel has been redone in a fashion that maintains original architecture while incorporating ultra-modern details. Rooms are spacious and designed with clean lines in mind. Décor jumps from modern minimalist to intricate stonework. It's a fun mix of yesterday and today and just the place to stay when you're looking for something very different. A fitness center and delicious dining opportunities at Harry's Bar & Grill make for a complete and convenient stay. If you're traveling with dogs, Magnolia Hotel has a very pet-friendly policy and all furry friends will be welcomed.

Chapter 12: Discovering Denver's Coffee Shops

Denver is a city that delivers plenty of options for green living and healthy eating. Functioning on a philosophy that there's generally a better way to approach life if only we would try, the coffee shops that reside in the Mile High City also benefit from this passionate way of thinking. It seems that around every corner there's a new, charming locale to be tried. Whether you crave caffeine or you're just looking for a place to pass a relaxing afternoon with friends, there are a few tasty coffee shops you'll want to try.

Pigtrain Coffee Company

1701 Wynkoop Street, Denver, Colorado 80202

A tasty highlight of any trip to Union Station, Pigtrain Coffee Company is a place to caffeinate and an entire experience in and of itself! Nearly always bustling, this is a great place to swing by and grab a seasonal latte alongside a scone or oversized cookie. Serving locally-brewed flavors and conscious coffee beans, you'll feel great knowing your java is served with a greater purpose. From cakes and macaroons to pain au chocolate Pigtrain nearly always has a snack of the day to accompany your beverage. If you're not in the mood for a coffee, try a smoothie or juice option. When the mood's right for something with a kick, the menu delivers alcohol infused coffee specialties. Stay and sip an espresso at the large wrap-around bar or make your way out to the exterior patio for some prime people watching. While you wait, the coffee bar has plenty of Pigtrain swag to keep you browsing and much of it highlights the history of Union Station.

Amante Coffee

1612 17th Street, Denver, Colorado 80202

A favorite along the Colorado Front Range with plans to expand, Amante provides a charming and authentically Italian experience when it comes to finding a place to sip an espresso in the city. Quaint in size and structure, you are guaranteed bold flavors every time you order. The 17th street location is particularly fun as it shares space with the historic Oxford Hotel. Along with a shot of caffeine, Amante makes pastries, paninis, scones and more available to customers. Sit by the window and watch the downtown world pass by or take it to go and find yourself dreaming of grand Italian escapes as you wander through Denver.

Mangiamo Pronto

1601 17th Street, Denver, Colorado 80202

A sister store to its well-loved Santa Fe counterpart, Mangiamo Pronto is a full-service restaurant by night and a caffeine lover's paradise by day. Known for their impeccable breakfast and all-day pizzas, Mangiamo also takes Italian coffee to an entirely new level. Their downtown location is close to Union Station making this a great stop before you get on the next train.

If you prefer your caffeinated beverages mild, this isn't the place for you. Mangiamo Pronto brings customers caffeine with a kick. You'll walk away from your espresso, cappuccino or latte with a lift of energy you didn't even know you needed. Since it's debut in 2009, Mangiamo Pronto continues to charm and inspire the residents of downtown Denver. A relaxing place to sit and people-watch from the patio, it's a must-try stop for coffee-lovers traveling through the city.

Novo

1600 Glenarm Place, Denver, Colorado 80202

A coffee shop unlike any other, Novo is a true Denver experience and a delicious side note to any given day of exploration. First opening their doors in 2002, this family-run coffee business has expanded to include 4 locations. While their coffee is crafted with a lot of love and care, it's the extras that take Novo above and beyond your average destination. Offering tours of their roastery and full tasting sessions on a weekly basis, the team at Novo encourages coffee drinkers to learn more about the beverage they love. The owners try to get out of town as often as possible and meet face-to-face with the individuals who are growing the beans they brew. Evidence of their travels is readily available to customers, giving all who step through their doors a face-to-face encounter with the entire coffee production process from start to finish. It's a unique opportunity to find a personal connection along with a great cup of joe.

Chapter 13: Majestic Mountain Excursions

Denver is most definitely a hub of urban growth and opportunity, but at its core, it's a place designed around the mountains. The city is captivating no matter what time of year you travel here but come when the snow begins to fall, and you'll find yourself in the midst of a passionate population pressing forward to Friday when they'll race to beat the rush to the slopes. It seems everyone here has a connection to the mountains and with good reason. The areas around Denver provide some of the best opportunities for skiing, snowboarding and tubing in the state. You don't have to drive far to make the most of what the mountains have to offer. Here are a few majestic highlights that make a ski trip to Denver magical.

Breckenridge

Breckenridge, Colorado 80424

A lively mountain community and a central hub for ski lovers across the state of Colorado, locals will refer to their trips to Breckenridge (Breck, as they lovingly call it) the millisecond there's a possibility for snow. Located only 1.5 hours from Denver via 70 West, it's hard to resist such a close call. Breckenridge is famous for it's Breck Effect, or that uniquely positive vibe that residents believe calls to those below and brings them up the mountain to experience wintery thrills at an exhilarating elevation of 12,840 ft.

With 5 peaks designating the Breckenridge area, skiers of all abilities will find a place to explore comfortable terrain, try some new skills and developing slope-side confidence. 187 trails to experience and 34 lifts to get you there means you'll never be out of things to do, try and see. Lessons for all levels, gear rental and lodging are available as long as the slopes are open, making a trip to Breckenridge both fun and convenient. Whether you come for a day or stay for a long weekend, Breckenridge brings the magic of the mountains and has a way of sticking with you long after you've left.

Vail

Vail, Colorado 81657

An easy two-miles east of Denver, high up in the peaks lies the iconic ski resort of Vail alongside with her charming villages. This quintessential ski town is the very definition of picturesque mountain escape and when winter hits, it becomes a hotbed of winter sports, outdoor concerts and snowy activity. Legendary terrain that provides the perfect assortment of slopes for beginner through expert-level skiers makes it a great stop when you're traveling with the whole family. It's a unique destination in that it's a fun place to visit even if you're not much for snow sports.

The village is primarily pedestrian-friendly and as the holidays close in, you'll find twinkling lights dotting cobblestone streets. As you make your way through, you can admire rustic buildings hosting restaurants, specialty shops and luxury hotels in between. There's even a central skate rink when you're ready to tie up those laces and hit the ice. Locals will be putting their Epic Season Passes to great use when the snow comes to Colorado, but visitors can easily purchase day or weekend passes depending on how much time you've set aside to ski and explore. Lessons are always available for newcomers and when you're here, make sure to check the events calendar for a look at the musical concert lineup as Vail hosts the infamous Vail Snow Days in December.

Winter Park

Winter Park, Colorado 80482

For over 75-years, Winter Park Ski Resort has been one of the ultimate destinations for locals and visitors hoping to make the most of the mountains during the snow, winter months. With seven designated territories making up the resort and over 3,081 acres waiting to be explored, it's no wonder those with a passion for hitting the slopes make their way to this renowned destination. Only 67 miles northwest of Denver, Winter Park is one of the closer ski destinations offering a diverse lineup when it comes to fun and entertainment. Expert skiers will love the runs on Vasquez Ridge that take them through challenging territory, often encountering loads of untouched powder on a daily basis. Families adore Winter Park for the progression of learning slopes available and lessons offered no matter when you come to play and stay. Winter Park web cams are available online so you have an idea of conditions before you even arrive. Once you do get here, you'll want to try everything and more. From tubing, dining, shopping and an incredible holiday market, Winter Park is a place that's perfect for skiers and snow adventurers alike.

Mountain-Bound Groups

While independent exploration can be exhilarating, if you're extremely new to mountain terrain, a better option can often be meeting up with groups that explore together or going the route of a guided tour. Fortunately, Denver offers both these options for those hoping to get out and see what the mountain scene is really all about.

Colorado Mountain Club has had its roots in Denver's outdoor culture since 1912. Created in the name of conservation and outdoor education, it's a great way for those who are new to mountainside exploration to meet up with those who have spent a lifetime high above the world below and adventure together. Guests can join the club for a fee and meet up for any or all excursions and planned events. Even if you're not a Colorado resident, joining the club means receiving regular and extremely educational information on how to approach the great outdoors. When you are in the area, you'll be able to participate in the more than 3,000 hikes and outdoor courses that are planned by the club, helping participants gain an in-depth understanding of what it means to appreciate and protect the natural gifts Colorado gives.

Colorado Sightseer is another local Denver group dedicated to providing customized outdoor tours of Denver and the surrounding mountain areas. With opportunities to explore year-round, these tours bring a personalized touch with knowledgeable guides, stops planned by locals that many other tour buses can't access as well as snacks and drinks included. It's a nice way to enjoy the mountain peaks and perks of Denver without feeling like you have to rush along with a group. Take your time, enjoy the view and ask all the questions you want. You'll walk away feeling invigorated and informed.

Jellystone Park

650 Sky View Ln. Larkspur, Colorado 80118

When you're in need of a mountain destination that highlights the best nature has to offer while maintaining the amenities, there's no better place than Jellystone. Based on the famous Yogi Bear cartoon, Jellystone Park in Larkspur, Colorado is a short 40-minute drive from Denver. An experience in what many would refer to as *glamping*, a stay at Jellystone is half kid-fun entertainment and half communing with nature all while relaxing in top-notch accommodations.

Themed weekends and heated pools bring a perfect balance for entertaining kids and adults alike. Feel free to hook up your RV or rent a cabin or cottage for the duration of your stay. If you go the cottage route, expect to find fully-equipped kitchens, spacious bedrooms and all the extras that make for comfortable living. A far cry from a rustic getaway, Jellystone lets you experience the outdoors alongside scheduled entertainment like gem-mining and a guarantee that you'll have a warm bed to welcome you when the sun sets.

Chapter 14: Theater, Stage and Performance

Travelers fall in love with Denver for reasons that span the inexplicable to the extremely personal. Whether it's a close relationship with the mountains, a passion for pushing the social limits or a sense of connection with a city that is booming in terms of population, Denver calls to people from across the globe. One of those things that Denver just gets right every time is the city's dedication to the arts. There's hardly a day that goes by without a show, festival or performance getting underway. In the name of all that is inspiring and creative, here are a few of Denver's best when it comes to the shining lights of the stage.

Paramount Theater

1621 Glenarm Pl. Denver, Colorado 80202

Seating approximately 1,870 guests, the Paramount Theater is a lively locale that features everyone from raunchy comedians to Kidz Bop concerts. It's just as fun to browse Paramount's lineup as it is to visit for a show due to the vast selection of shows and genre available. This multi-level performance hall is adorned with bold interior décor and ornate ceiling paintings that remind one of a trip to the theater in the early 20th century. Complete with full concession services and a neon sign that lights the way from outside, you won't want to miss a chance to enjoy a show or concert at Paramount Theater when you're in town.

The Denver Performing Arts Complex

1400 Curtis Street, Denver, Colorado 80204

The theater district of downtown Denver is primarily made up of a massive 4-block center known as The Denver Performing Arts Complex. Connected by an intricate overhead awning and a multi-level parking garage, the complex is a maze of theaters hosting a variety of performances year-round. With a collection of theaters big enough to dazzle guests with visions of Broadway's best performances right next to small stages tucked away in an intimate, more charming setting—there is much to see and do in this lively area of town. If you've booked tickets for a show, plan on coming a little early and make the most of the complex's dining and drinking options at the Limelight Supper Club & Lounge. This is the absolute best place to be when you're craving a night out on the town. From Opera to Alternative rock and every Broadway and Off-Broadway show between, The Denver Performing Arts Complex is a haven of creative showmanship.

Film On The Rocks

18300 W Alameda Pkwy. Morrison, Colorado 80465

Red Rocks Amphitheatre is known for hosting some of the biggest names in the music business. However, it's also an incredible place to visit in the summertime for a chance to enjoy an outdoor movie! Between May and August, the venue opens up to guest around 6:30 pm on designated nights. Visitors are treated to a musical guest and a comedian before being settling in to enjoy a big screen movie production when dusk falls. The event is a collaboration between Denver Arts & Venues and the Denver Film Society. Since it's inauguration in 2017 thousands have attended and there's no end in sight for this once in a lifetime opportunity for movie lovers.

88 Drive In Theatre

8780 Rosemary Street, Commerce City, Colorado 80022

Denver's gift for preserving the past extends into its love for the cinematic arts as well. The ultimate trip through movie time history is available just outside of Denver. A stop at 88 Drive In Theatre is a way of honoring the past and having a blast while you're at it. This family-run outdoor theater has been in the Denver area since 1972 and has no intention of going away any time soon.

Welcoming guests throughout the summer months, the giant projector gives way to all the latest flicks every night of the week. Come early to park according to car size and simply tune in to the drive-in station for a surround sound experience right from your vehicle. Many families bring outdoor gear such as frisbees and footballs to make a night of it on the large field in front of the screen before the film even starts. A small concession building serves up pizza, popcorn, cotton candy along with several other goodies and souvenirs to give your night a tasty twist. Compared to the price of a standard theater experience, a night at 88 Drive In constitutes a real steal. For just $8.00 guests can enjoy three full-length movies before departing for home in the wee hours of the morning!

AMC Highlands Ranch 24

103 Centennial Blvd. Highlands Ranch, Colorado 80129

Movie-going is a time-honored tradition and Denver offers up some exceptional venues for viewing the latest and greatest in cinematic marvels. While it may not offer up the historic value of a drive-in theater, the AMC Highlands Ranch 24 is a sprawling cinema complex that delivers high on the modern movie experience scale. The theater itself provides dual level parking and a covered walk-way leading to escalators directing you towards the main doors. Considering Denver's unexpected weather patterns, this comes in as a handy extra more often than not.

Once inside, you'll marvel at the sheer size of the building surrounding you. More than your standard theater, AMC Highlands Ranch 24 brings guests the convenience of pre-heated, ready to grab popcorn, a full-service snack bar and a create your own drinks station. Mix and match your drinks and snacks until your hearts content. If you're in the mood for something a bit stronger, there's a bar just across from the arcade. For movie-goers who are passionate about choice, this location comes complete with IMAX, Dolby Cinema and RealD 3D alongside standard viewing formats.

When it comes to convenience, this theater complex reigns supreme. Tickets and seating can be reserved online with the click of a button taking the hassle out of arrival times or searching for just the right seat. The same can be said for snacks! Order your food and drinks online ahead of time and simply pick them up from the counter once you get there. The theaters are modern and spacious with seats that nearly fully recline. Gone are the days of straight-backed film experiences. At AMC Highlands Ranch 24, you have all the convenience of home right there is a theater ready to serve up the delicious extras alongside an amazing movie.

Chapter 15: Venues with a View

When you come to Denver for work or play, there is a tendency to rush in the name of all there is to see and do. From the bustling downtown scene to the outlying mountain excursions, it's easy to find oneself sprinting from place to place in order to make the most of your time in the city and surrounding areas. While you're in the Mile High City, take a moment to remind yourself to sit back and enjoy as well. In recent years Denver has sprawled into an urban space to be reckoned with, but there is still so much beauty to be admired. Between the rising cityscape and the looming mountains is a view that beckons you to recognize just how stunning this city truly is. Here are a few places to make time to visit in the name of sitting down, if only for a moment and truly admiring this incredible place you've traveled so far to see.

Inspiration Point Park

4901 Sheridan Blvd. Denver, Colorado 80212

The inspiration for this park was first voiced back in 1906 when a gentleman by the name of Charles Mulford Robinson recognized a need for a space where people to come to witness the city's progress from above. Today, Inspiration Point Park is still one of the best places in the city to view panoramic landscapes that include Denver's urban sprawl alongside the awe-inspiring Front Range.

This 25-acre bluff-top destination is a peaceful place to take a moment to simply reflect on what's before you. Leisurely wander the winding, paved pathways enjoying the view, or stop to admire the many well-groomed flower beds that are scattered throughout the park. Strategically-placed benches give you a spot to sit and take advantage of this heightened location while simultaneously feeling very much a part of this drastically changing landscape.

Denver International Airport

8500 Peña Blvd, Denver, Colorado 80249

When you're flying into Denver International Airport, remind yourself to take a moment to take advantage of that view out the window. No matter what direction you arrive from, flying into Denver provides stunning mountaintop views that never cease to thrill. Ever-changing weather patterns mean a new and dramatic scene no matter what's happening in the sky as you get ready to land. Rainy days provide an interesting landing through fog as mountains suddenly appear before you in a spectacular show of surprise. Clear and sunny days give you the ability to see the Front Range and beyond stretching for miles into the distance. It's an incredible sight and one you don't want to miss.

Beyond the view from the interior of the plane, Denver International Airport is a really great place for collecting a memorable vantage point all on its own. With a central terminal made in a tent-like fashion to resemble the mountains, a walk around or through the airport gives you a fun comparison point as the real mountains and airport mimic one another. These bold designs and architectural statements alongside the beauty of the surrounding natural world make for a must-see view, pleasing several million passengers traveling through each year.

Peaks Lounge

650 15th Street, Denver, Colorado 80202

Just because you're looking for the most natural view of Denver doesn't mean it can't be done with class and style. When you're craving the best vantage point and perhaps a cocktail on the side, make your way towards the downtown Hyatt Regency and hurry up to the 27th floor. It's here that you'll be introduced to Peaks Lounge and all the perks that come along with it.

Floor to ceiling windows accompany ultra-modern décor and provide the perfect setting to soak up the panoramic views of the Rocky Mountains that surround you. The full-service bar keeps your glass full while you sit back and enjoy the fact that you're experiencing the city from one of the most admired vantage points available. Settle in bar-side to sip the night away or take a table closer to the windows for the thrilling sensation only a 27-floor height difference between land and sky can create.

Chapter 16: Athletic Intrigue-- Denver's Best Sporting Stops

The city of Denver draws sports fans in relentlessly and there's a good reason why. With top-tier teams in basketball, football and baseball, there's a reason to get out and support athletes across the board in Colorado. With so much athletic appeal, Denver is a great place to come and let your team's flag fly proudly. Here are a few places that host some of Denver's most well-loved teams and make for a fun day as a sports fan in the city.

Coors Field-Colorado Rockies

2001 Blake Street, Denver, Colorado 80205

When it comes to the Major Leagues, Denver has made Coors Field home for their much-loved Colorado Rockies. Located directly in the heart of downtown, this field is a fun and spacious place to spend game day. Since its opening in 1995 this location has been dazzling fans by the thousands. Sporting views of the Rocky Mountains from multi-level vantage points, it's a place that brings the scenic advantage alongside great baseball.

You'll want to spend some time wandering before you take your seat. Coors Field comes complete with a number of dining and beverage options that make for a tasteful afternoon out. The Sandlot Brewery brings you the flavor of local brews right inside the stadium.

The Jack Daniel's Terrace Bar gives you the freedom to enjoy the game while savoring craft beers or customized cocktails from the upper heights of the stadium. With large screens placed throughout the entirety of the stadium and so many delicious options along the way, you'll quickly find a day at Coors Field goes beyond a standard game of baseball. Make sure you arrive early to make the most of the fun. The field's downtown location is exciting, but also makes for some tricky parking that tends to fill up fast.

Mile High Stadium-Denver Broncos

1701 Bryant Street, Denver, Colorado 80204

Denver sits at a well-recognized elevation of 5,280 feet making it appropriately named the Mile High City. In honor of its elevated station on the map, Denver has also given the name to it's most beloved football team's home base. The Denver Broncos call Mile High Stadium home and this impressive location is a breathtaking stop for many fans.

If you're a die-hard Broncos fans, you'll want to be sure to book tickets well in advance. Its central location makes parking a bit of a hassle and you may want to arrive early to make sure you have a spot. The stadium is an impressive feat of steel and glass and gives the impression of grandeur long before you reach the front doors. Once inside, visitors enjoy views of the mountains and downtown Denver. Built to accommodate 76,125 people, this stadium quickly transforms into a frenzy of excitement and fun!

If you don't have the time to stay for an entire game, consider booking a stadium tour on a day when the Broncos aren't in town to play. Tours are approximately an hour and a half long and are built to please guests of all ages. Friendly and informative guides will take you through the stadium and include a chance to discover the Colorado Sports Hall of Fame and Museum. From game day to any given day of the week, Mile High Stadium is a great place to immerse yourself in the football culture of Denver.

Pepsi Center-Denver Nuggets

1000 Chopper Circle, Denver, Colorado 80204

The Pepsi Center is a well-known venue for music lovers in Denver as much of the year is dedicated to an incredible line up of concerts and performances. However, when basketball season rolls around, Pepsi Center transforms into the heart and soul of the Denver Nuggets. Multifunctional and easy to access, the Pepsi Center is the perfect place to catch a game and grab a hotdog when you're looking for a fantastic afternoon of athletic showmanship.

Featuring five levels and a spacious layout no matter where your seats are located, the center is unique in that it also holds designated practice space for the teams it hosts. While the Denver Nuggets are well-known in the world of Basketball, Pepsi Center also houses the Colorado Mammoth and Colorado Avalanche when it's time for ice-based sports to take center stage. Complete with luxury seat and theater box options, Pepsi Center is a prime location for sporting events and family-friendly shows no matter what season you're traveling through Denver.

The REI Denver Flagship Store

1416 Platte Street, Denver, Colorado 80202

When you're in Denver and have a passion for all-things athletic, the option to indulge in what you love goes well beyond stadiums and fields. In fact, a trip to the REI Denver flagship store is a satisfying adventure in discovering just how seriously the people of Denver take their sports and outdoor endeavors. Accommodating athletes of all ages and skill levels, the REI Denver flagship store is an impressive location dedicated to sporting gear, classes, excursions and much more!

Whether you're an expert in paddling, climbing, skiing, running, hiking or camping, REI delivers top-tier equipment and gear alongside a knowledgeable staff that's always ready and waiting to offer up sports-specific advice and insight. Buy your gear on the spot or go the rental route if you're heading to the mountains during your travels. Avid cyclists will be pleased to find a full-service bike shop available with skiers and snowboarder receiving equal treatment and services!

If you're more interested in participating in an REI sponsored event, there's plenty to choose from. An ever-growing list of activities includes introductions to snow shoeing as well as rock climbing classes. First aid classes are an important follow up to your mountain biking class. Hosting a variety of sports-themed classes and activities, there's sure to be a selection for every athlete in the family.

Chapter 17: Denver and the Divine

Denver is generally regarded as a city where open minds thrive. The same can be said for the spiritual scene. As diverse as the population who calls Denver home, there are a variety of churches to choose from when you're traveling through Denver and looking for places of worship. Here are a few stops to consider visiting when you're looking for a Sunday morning service in Denver.

Flatirons Community Church

2700 S Downing Street, Denver, Colorado 80210

Based out of Lafayette, Colorado, Flatirons Community Church is a non-denominational house of worship that takes a modern approach towards the idea of remaining inclusive while retaining the title of mega church. Hosting thousands of visitors weekly from Colorado and across the globe, Flatirons uses their headquarters in Lafayette to live broadcast their messages to five other campuses holding services at the same time. Denver's campus on South Downing Street offers up an intimate setting for visitors in what was once a brown-brick facade Presbyterian church. One you walk inside the atmosphere changes drastically.

While the building still hosts the gorgeous stained-glass windows, lower floor and balcony as well as a towering ceiling with exposed beams, a full concert-worthy stage has been set up for live music and a massive screen is used to project the main message. Lights, fog machines and special effects are all common on the Sunday morning lineup. Both modern Christian and original music sets grace the stage at Flatirons and the worship team is well-versed in secular music, often bringing current hits to Sunday service in a way that integrates in some way with the message of the day.

Visitors are invited to grab a coffee and a free Bible before making their way to their seats. Flatirons also live broadcasts their service on YouTube for those who can't physically get to one of their locations on a Sunday. Utilizing all the resources technology provides, this is a church that calls to many Denver residents and continues to grow.

Potter's House Church of Denver

9495 E Florida Avenue, Denver, Colorado 80247

If you're looking for a church on Sunday morning in Denver that brings high-energy and puts gospel music center stage, Potter's House Church of Denver is the place for you. This urban mega church hosts several thousand visitors on a weekly basis and falls under the denomination category of *independent*. Born out of the vision of a parent church based in Dallas, Potter's House Church of Denver brings the Sunday morning extras to another level.

Children can be dropped off at a full-service daycare complete with musical programing and a gift shop full of toys to browse when service is done. Adults can mingle in the spacious lobby before the music gets started or stop by the café and pick up a coffee for that morning kick of energy. Visitors will appreciate the parking lot attendants that lead new guests to priority parking spaces set aside just for newcomers. Once inside, no need to worry about getting lost as there are several people walking around to help guide the way to children's ministries and help adults get seated in the large auditorium. Committed to their diverse crowd, Potter's House Church of Denver offers services in Spanish as well.

Cathedral Basilica of the Immaculate Conception

1530 Logan Street, Denver, Colorado 80203

This stunning and divine landmark of Denver first opened its doors in 1911 and to this day, remains an incredible place to visit and admire as well as a lovely place to worship if you are a follower of the Catholic faith. Mass is held daily as well as hosting five masses on Sunday. Visitors and worshipers alike will want to stop and admire the vast central nave complete with towering stone columns, 75 windows of stained-glass and impressive upper-level organ echoing music along the many passage ways.

A location dedicated to reflection and reunion with God, the cathedral is a masterful work of art that sends spires reaching into the sky and provides those passing by with an ornate and intricate stone facade. The cathedral regularly hosts concerts and has even been known to have a movie night or two. The Cathedral Basilica of the Immaculate Conception provides for the less fortunate in the city of Denver by opening its doors to the homeless and hungry and providing lunches and dines on a routine basis.

Chapter 18: Stopping for a Drink Along the Way

Let's face it, touring a new city is exciting but it comes with it's fair share of stress. Between the spotty GPS, making sure the whole family sticks together and that inevitable wrong turn you're bound to make there are a lot of moments that could lead to a negative turning point. When you reach these travel moments in Denver, it's important to remember that this is a city built on flavor. From breweries to bars, Denver has a way with taste that's easily served up in a glass. Whether you're passionate about wine or itching to find the best local brew, here are a few places guaranteed to please and take the edge off travel tension while you're at it.

Terminal Bar

1701 Wynkoop Street, Denver, Colorado 80211

Brining the upscale atmosphere to the heart of downtown Denver, Terminal Bar is chic and convenient place to sit and sip your way through an afternoon or evening. Taking up a significant portion of the newly renovated Union Station, Terminal Bar gives you a place to cozy up and watch the world hustle by on their way to catching a train.

Seating options are spectacular as you have the choice of making your way into the bar area where plush booths create charming locations to land in darkened corners. Have a seat and order some small plates to go along with your drink or side up the bar and have a chat with the bartender instead. Once you've ordered, you're not locked into the booth scene. Go ahead and make your way around the corner once more and find a place along one of the many wooden benches that keeps you close enough to chat, but conveniently central for great people-watching opportunities! Standing tables are scattered around the outer edges of Terminal Bar as well for those moments you don't intend to linger or just want to stretch after a day of travel.

The beverage menu at Terminal Bar is vast and varied. Draught beer, signature cocktails and wine by the glass are all a part of the Terminal Bar package. Take your time deciding but keep in mind that the Wynkoop Sour comes highly recommended. If you're being mindful of a budget, take advantage of Terminal Bar's Happy Hour which runs Monday through Friday from 4 pm to 6 pm and brings a glass of wine down to $7.00.

Thirsty Lion Gastropub & Grill

1605 Wynkoop Street, Denver, Colorado 80202

Just down the street from Union Station is a fun and lively hang out where you can linger at the bar, cozy into a booth or make your way to a high-top table to enjoy a delicious beverage. Thirsty Lion Gastropub & Grill is a popular place due to its prime downtown location and proximity to Union Station. If you come on a weekend, it's advisable to make a reservation so you can skip the line of eager guests and make your way directly to a table.

This location is a sprawling building filled from end to end with seating options. Large-screen televisions adorn the central bar to broadcast big games. It's hard to find a time of day when Thirsty Lion isn't a popular place to be. High ceilings and floor to ceiling windows give you a view of the bustling outside world at all hours. While Thirsty Lion is known for great dinner menu items, many locals frequent this hub for the benefits of Happy Hour. For just $4.95 you can savor the house wines, well drinks and delicious margaritas between the hours of 3pm and 6pm as well as 9:30 pm until close every night of the week! Pair your purchase up with a yummy started item. While everything is tasty, the soft pretzel and variety of dipping sauces along with the Spinach and Artichoke dip make for a great way to spend the evening.

Falling Rock Tap House

1919 Blake Street, Denver, Colorado 80202

Perhaps the ultimate destination when it comes to grabbing a drink and catching the game, Falling Rock Tap House brings a casual atmosphere along with the ultimate selection of draft beers to downtown Denver. A large bar as well as a variety of comfortable couches and plush booths make for easy seating options upon arrival. While this location does offer up food option, it's the beer that brings in the fans. Boasting over 75 beers on tap, you'll be met with a wall of spouts and an awe-inspiring choice to make when it comes to flavor. A well-loved downtown locale with fun staff, a cool vibe and plenty of people to meet along the way, Falling Rock Tap House is a great stop for those with a passion for the brew.

Skyline Beer Garden

1601 Arapahoe Street, Denver, Colorado 80202

If you're looking for an amazing place to not only grab a drink, but make an entire afternoon of it, then Skyline Beer Garden is the place to be. This sprawling green space is a unique pop-up in the middle of downtown and takes up 3 city-blocks. While it was created in the spirit of celebrating all that is fantastic about Colorado and craft beer, the location brings entertainment alongside savory delights in a glass.

Skyline Beer Garden is easily accessible and offers visitors a chance to grab a drink and play the afternoon away. Complete with miniature golf, ping pong and corn hole, guests can feel free to move between flavors and fun! If you're in the mood to sit and chat, find your way to one of the many benches and watch as others take competitive corn hole to another level. Street-style food is readily available at this location including tacos, nachos and tasty desserts. If you're willing to linger, Skyline Beer Garden hosts live music many nights of the week. A flavorful stop with much more to offer in the way of entertainment, this is a great place to come with friends or family when you're in Denver.

Marg's World Taco Bistro

500 E 19th Avenue, Denver, Colorado 80203

Sometimes, there's nothing like a flavorful south of the boarder experience to bring you back to life after a long day of sightseeing. Marg's is the answer to all of those bold and savory questions you been asking as you've maneuvered your way through downtown Denver. From house specialty salsa to tender pork belly and all the world class tacos in between, Marg's is a must-try for dinner time happiness. While the food is good, it's always been the drink list that puts Marg's over the top. Mixing top of the line Tequila with fanciful flavors such as grapefruit, watermelon, mint and habanero—there's nothing quite like an afternoon margarita at Marg's to make your day a bit more exciting.

If you lean more towards the vodka or whiskey way of life, not to worry, Marg's has you covered here as well. Try the Whiskey Smash which brings a combination of grapefruit, lime and orange into a new light or put a minty spin on your evening with a Marg's Mojito. The Larceny Buck features a smooth blend of lemon and Bourbon while the Cucumber+Basil brings out the best in a vodka and agave mix-up.

Chapter 19: A Trip Through Colorado Springs

A mere 71-miles south of Denver is a place as alluring as the Mile High city itself. Easily accessible via I-25, the drive to Colorado Springs is a rather straight shot and always brings scenic pleasures. As the front range gives way to taller peaks of the eastern Rocky Mountains, Colorado Springs comes into view. This stunning and diverse city is close enough to call itself Denver's neighbor while maintaining an exciting identity all its own. An awe-inspiring combination of unique land formations and formidable slopes that include Pikes Peak- Colorado Springs is worth setting aside some time to visit when you're traveling in and around Denver.

Compassion International

12290 Voyager Parkway, Colorado Springs, Colorado 80921

What began as a single man's effort to save 35 orphans in South Korea in 1952 has blossomed into one of the largest child advocacy organizations in the United States today. Compassion International is a ministry-based organization that allows individuals to sponsor children in poverty across the globe. Fundraising efforts and donor giving provide the foundation for Compassion International to build and staff child development centers in the areas hardest hit by misfortune. Children who are sponsored and attend Compassion's development centers are provided opportunities for food, education and skills acquisition specific to their community potential. Family members often accompany children to these lessons, fostering a sense of commitment to independence.

The Compassion International headquarters is locating in a sprawling complex right in the heart of Colorado Springs and is open for touring for those who are interested. Hosting 1-hour long tours three times a day, visitors simply park in the visitor parking lot and make their way towards the main entrance. The tours are designed to show guests how children live and learn in the countries where most sponsorship is happening. Tour a replica of a child development center and witness the processing center where thousands of donor and child letters are processed and sent regularly. Calling in advance gives you a chance to organize a child-specific tour or set up a private tour for you and your family. Either way, a stop at Compassion International is an incredible insider-look at how this massive organization grew from its foundation, functions on a daily basis and currently thrives in Colorado and around the world.

United States Air Force Academy

2304 Cadet Drive, US Air Force Academy, Colorado 80840

One of the highlights of visiting Colorado Springs is participating in an official tour of the United States

Air Force Academy. A central hub of military training and technical advancement, the academy brings up cadets in the way of protecting the country via air channels and visitors are always welcome to come and have a guided look around. The Barry Goldwater Airforce Academy Visitor Center opened in 1986 and is where your tour will begin. Guests can expect to experience a short film highlighting academy achievements and taking a closer look at what cadet life is really all about.

Moving on from the theater, the tour will include a chance to browse several exhibits which bring the history of the U.S. Air Force Academy to life. The Air Force Academy hosts its own football team, band and choir. Calling in advance to reserve a tour time can help give you a bit more access to some of these points of academy interest including the stadium. With a history and culture rich in academic success and military pride, a tour of the United States Air Force Academy isn't just for prospective students. Complete with stunning mountain backdrops and covering an impressive expanse of land, it's a place where visitors from all walks of life can stop by to appreciate the training behind the talent of the armed forces with an up-close look at active training facilities.

The Broadmoor

1 Lake Avenue, Colorado Springs, Colorado 80906

The Broadmoor is one of Colorado's premier getaway resorts and it's located right in the heart of scenic

Colorado Springs. Elegant, spacious and sprawling over well-groomed lawns, this well-loved location opened its door in 1918 and has been enchanting guests ever since. Taking the natural wonder of the mountains and canyons, The Broadmoor gives guests a luxurious experience in the western way of life.

Much more than just a chic night away, a stay at the Broadmoor tantalizes the senses. Guests have the freedom to choose between adrenaline pumping activities or a day lounging away in a top-class spa. Between the horseback riding, dips in the large, pristine pool, ziplining, tennis and golf, guests will work up quite the appetite. Fortunately, the Broadmoor brings the best in world-class dining opportunities. A variety of on-site restaurants and cafes guarantees there's something on the menu to please. From upscale French cuisine to Italian fare with a Colorado twist, visitors to the Broadmoor are delivered exquisite flavors and bold options when it comes to finding just the right meal to satisfy your hunger.

Garden of the Gods

1805 N 30th Street, Colorado Springs, Colorado 80904

This Colorado Springs landmark is a must-see when you're in the area. A collection of towering sandstone spiked peaks, Garden of the Gods is a perfect way to stay within the boundaries of Colorado Springs but feel like you've been transported to another planet.

These land formations are captivating and in combination with the mountains that surround them, create for a truly unforgettable view. Photographers who want to capture the essence won't have to look far, with awe-inspiring views just about every direction you turn.

Visitors with a passion for rock climbing, hiking or off-road adventure will appreciate the opportunities to explore on the ground or from above. If you're interested in learning to climb or hike some of those more challenging trails, guided tours and private lessons are available. Those who are more in the mood to just admire the scenery can take advantage of the smooth, paved trails that wind in between the rocks and give you a close-up view of their incredible beauty. Make sure to stop by the Visitor and Nature Center while you're here for some educational insight on the history of the park and how it became a national landmark. This is also a great place to get information on upcoming events at Garden of the Gods including educational programs that dig into the dinosaurs that once ruled this area as well as tribal performances and ceremonies.

Chapter 20: Seasonal Stops

Denver delivers big on fun, entertainment and food, but there's something special about visiting the city during the holidays. Denver's ever-growing population means that with each passing year, there seems to be an equally exciting growth on the seasonal stops list. From holiday light spectaculars to farms that beckon Denver's population to make the most of the autumn chill, here are a few places to put on the itinerary when you're heading towards Denver during those big-name celebrations.

Downtown Christmas Market

1515 Arapahoe Street, Denver, Colorado 80202

Officially titled the Denver Christkindl Market, this yearly experience in seasonal shopping, dining and live entertainment is much loved by those who frequent downtown Denver. Located on the 16th Street Mall, this market is a pedestrian-friendly experience in browsing seasonal souvenirs, charming crafts and arts as well as trying something sweet. Running from mid-November through late December, this downtown holiday market is a place to cozy up with your loved one and try some authentic European pastries alongside a warming hot chocolate. For those who have a passion for beer any time of year, a large selection of labels are highlighted during this festival time.

Holiday markets are a centuries-old tradition in Germany and the festival's flawless and fun history in Denver is attributed to the efforts of the German American Chamber of Commerce. Excited to share these traditions from home with those who flock to Denver, the Christkindl Market is a place to enjoy culture, try something new and make the most of the season by celebrating with friends and family.

Parker Trick or Treat on Mainstreet

20000 Pikes Peak Avenue, Parker, Colorado 80138

Denver does Halloween right...mostly for adults. From downtown zombie parades to music festivals with a dark twist, Denver is the perfect place to be if you're a fan of Halloween and don't mind activities that come with a side of creepy. However, for those traveling with kids who are looking for a more family-friendly event, Parker is a right next-door option that brings all the fun in an easy to access atmosphere.

Just a 20-minute drive from city center, Parker hosts the annual Trick or Treat on Mainstreet event that brings big city dwellers to the outskirts of Denver in droves. Families love this event because it delivers big on candy for the kids but doesn't require too much foot traffic once you've arrived. Mainstreet is entirely shut down for pedestrian-only traffic and guests are invited to arrive in costume as they make their way from store to store and trick or treat the night away! While this is great fun for the little ones it's also an incredible opportunity for local businesses to highlight their wares. Don't be surprised to find a few coupons for a free ice cream or a discounted hand-painted mug in your Halloween goodies. Supporting the local community and providing a safe place for Halloween fun makes Parker the perfect place to trick or treat when you're traveling through Denver during October.

Anderson Farms

6728 County Road 3 ¼ Erie, Colorado 80516

Just outside of Denver in rustic Erie, Colorado lies a majestic and sprawling plot of land designed to bring visitors the best of autumn. What's better than a trip to the pumpkin patch when the leaves start to change colors and there's that very specific chill in the air? The staff at Anderson Farms doesn't think there's anything that beats it and as a way to celebrate the season, transforms their entire agricultural space into a Fall Festival beginning in mid-September.

Guests have the chance to take a wagon ride out to one of the several, massive pumpkin fields and choose their favorites by hand. Ride back to one of the cashier barns to weigh your goods and maybe purchase some sweets or handmade household items before you move along. Once the pumpkins are picked, kids are free to run wild and make the most of the intricate on-site corn maze, roast marshmallows around a campfire or play the day away on the jungle gym or tire castle! Older kids will enjoy playing zombie paintball or taking a turn launching pumpkins from a canon. With something fun for everyone in the family, you'll come in the name of fall but remember your time at Anderson Farms for years after your visit.

Chapter 21: Last Minute Tips and Tricks

Being a Mindful Tourist

Like any large city, Denver is a place that welcomes tourism and residents are excited to share their space of creative energy, innovative thoughts and passion that is constantly being balanced between the city and mountains. When you're here, be sure to be mindful of the places where these values and interests collide. It's not uncommon to see business attire and ski gear walking side by side when you're downtown. You'll frequently find everyday establishments such as gas stations or coffee shops lined up next to Cannabis clinics. Denver is a city that fluctuates in rhythm, structure and reasoning. With its growing population, construction is a current way of life with no quick end in sight and while sightseeing, you're sure to stumble upon massive numbers of scaffolding or re-routing notices.

Denver is a city where change is embraced and with so many changes happening in the city right now, it's important to be mindful of how you as an individual tourist approach the city's well-being. Being in-tune to the daily dynamic, ever-changing traffic patterns and creative influences will allow you to appreciate this diverse city while also protecting yourself.

When you're traveling with family, take the hassle out of downtown parking by considering a trip on the Lite Rail. Be sure to find time to visit those major destinations during the day but if you're considering trying something new, don't be shy about setting up guided visits. Denver is a city that encourages trying new things in life, but you should also take advantage of the experts who thrive in this city and are here to help. Whether you're here for the food, the shows, the night life or the family-fun, Denver is a great place to explore and experience. Taking time to understand and appreciate the dynamics that make Denver different will give you a more thorough view of your vacation and keep you coming back to learn more.

Living with the Lite Rail

The past several years has seen Denver's city rail line known as the Lite Rail grow beyond belief. Convenient, budget friendly and easy to use, the Lite Rail is part of Denver's greater RTD Bus and Rail system that serves the entire city. The Lite Rail in particular moves an ever-growing population from place to place while eliminating the hassle of driving in Denver and helping keep the city's air quality at acceptable levels. The trains currently run on nine lines and include 53 stops throughout the city.

The lines are divided between four zones with each zone requiring a specific fare. Zones A and B will cost travelers $2.60 per ride while including zone C on a ticket raises the price to $4.50. Zone D is considered Denver International Airport and as of only a few years ago, those looking for an easy route to DIA can simply hop on the airport train at Union Station. $9.00 will get you there in about 45 minutes with convenient luggage racks included for a hands-free ride. Buying your ticket is as simple as a stop at one of the ticket vending machines hosted at every station. In most cases there are multiple to choose from so you don't need to wait in line. Buy a pass for the day or for a single ride depending on your plans and leave the car at home.

About the Expert

Caitlyn Knuth is a lifelong writer who was inspired to put a pen to paper as a child long before spelling skills were acquired. Constantly captivated by the pictures words have the power to paint and the owner of a spirit that is always ready for the next travel adventure, she's found her muse alive and well through the process of exploring new cities and sharing what she's found with the world.

After accepting a job in Denver several years ago, she made it her mission to learn as much about this very new, exciting and eccentric city as possible in an effort to somehow make it home a bit more quickly. With a plan in place to try something new every weekend, it didn't take long to become captivated with all there was to see and do in the Mile High City. Before long, she had acquired a list of incredible stops to try and sights to see that made up a collection of stories begging to be told.

Armed with this wealth of new information, a passion for adventure and a never-ending list of must-try places to pass onto others, she decided to put together a comprehensive guide to the version of Denver she has learned to love.

HowExpert publishes quick 'how to' guides on unique topics by everyday experts. Visit <u>HowExpert.com</u> to learn more.

Recommended Resources

www.HowExpert.com – Quick 'How To' Guides on Unique Topics by Everyday Experts.

www.HowExpert.com/writers - Write About Your #1 Passion/Knowledge/Experience.

www.HowExpert.com/membership - Learn a New 'How To' Topic About Practically Everything Every Week.

www.HowExpert.com/jobs - Check Out HowExpert Jobs.

Made in the USA
San Bernardino,
CA